THE DOG & THE FEVER

Wesleyan University Press

Middletown CT 06459

www.wesleyan.edu/wespress

Manufactured in the United States of America

Designed by Mindy Basinger Hill

Typeset in Adobe Caslon Pro

Library of Congress Cataloging-in-Publication Data

Names: Espinosa, Pedro, 1578–1650 author. | Williams,
William Carlos, 1883–1963 translator author of commentary |
Williams, Raquel Hélène Rose Hoheb, 1847–1949 translator |
Cohen, Jonathan, 1949 May 4– editor | Mariani, Paul L.
author of foreword

Title: The dog and the fever: a perambulatory novella /
Pedro Espinosa; translated from the Spanish by William
Carlos Williams with Raquel Hélène Williams; commentary
by William Carlos Williams; edited and with an introduction
by Jonathan Cohen; foreword by Paul Mariani.

Other titles: Perro y la calentura. English

Description: Middletown, Conn.:
Wesleyan University Press, 2018. |
Includes bibliographical references.

Identifiers: LCCN 2017046021| ISBN 9780819578044
(cloth: alk. paper) | ISBN 9780819578037 (pbk.: alk. paper)

Classification: LCC PQ6390.E6 P4713 2018 | DDC 863/.3—dc23
LC record available at https://lccn.loc.gov/2017046021

5   4   3   2   1

CONTENTS

*Visit Wesleyan's website for various documents related to this book,
including the original Spanish text (modern spelling), the 1625
and 1736 Spanish editions, the 1707 English translation, and the uncut
version of William Carlos Williams's commentary on the novella:
wesleyan.edu/wespress/readerscompanions*

ACKNOWLEDGMENTS

I must express my gratitude to the Spanish artist Vicente Castelló (1815–72) for his engravings that appear as illustrations in this book; Francisco López Estrada for his scholarly work on Pedro Espinosa; friends and colleagues Marjorie Agosín, Daniel Deutsch, Yolanda Gamboa, Edith Grossman, Paul Mariani, Julio Marzán, Gy Mirano, Antonio Muñoz Molina, Victoriano Roncero-López, and Bill Zavatsky for their encouragement, critical insights, or both; and my wife, Ellen Lerner, for her help with the work and for all her loving support.

—JONATHAN COHEN—

In the Everyday Idiom of Spain

The Dog and the Fever is a fantastic piece of work, and I can see many reasons why William Carlos Williams was taken by it, especially by the sense of the language that Pedro Espinosa got down on the page. It is Williams himself listening to the living language around him there in Rutherford or Paterson or Manhattan and then working to get what he heard—the music of it!—likewise down on the page. Both men heard not the courtly or academic but the living vulgate, and the poetry intrinsic to that. What's also fascinating about Williams's translation is the way he tries to find the modern idiomatic equivalent for a language harking back three hundred years and more, then transmuted through Caribbean idioms, where it was picked up by his mother, who in the 1930s, in her eighties, transmitted the living Spanish idiom to her son with the pithy, vibrant language of her Puerto Rican background.

It becomes increasingly clear with the passing of time that, to more fully understand Williams's achievement as an American poet, we must understand just how deeply his Spanish heritage and the Spanish language enter into our understanding of what he himself called the American idiom, both the North and the South of it. And what Williams has given us in his translation of *The Dog and the Fever*—written in the wake of the Spanish Civil

War—is a fresh, crisp sense of Spain at the height of the Spanish Empire. It's especially striking that he should find in this text an example of *conceptismo* and its use of the slangy, everyday idiom of Spain—the language as it was actually spoken—that reinforced the very thing he himself was attempting to do in his own epic of America, *Paterson*.

The satire of *The Dog and the Fever* is heady, hilarious, witty, scathing, and ironic, and it captures something of the language that the average citizen of New York City, say, needs, to survive. Williams found words in the African-American idiom and the everyday language of Italian Americans that he introduced into his epic: interwoven strands of the river of language gathering above the Passaic Falls. By adding Williams's own comments from his letters and *Autobiography* as well as comments he added to the manuscript drafts of the novella, Jonathan Cohen has given us a much better sense of how Williams's Spanish heritage and his lifelong interest in Spanish and Latin American poetry enter into his complex epic. And that's the point: to more fully understand Williams's achievement as perhaps the foremost twentieth-century poet writing in the American grain.

When I read my own poems and spoke on Williams for the anniversary of the founding of Paterson back in the 1990s, alongside Allen Ginsberg, Jimmy Santiago Baca, Sonia Sanchez, Robert Creeley, Amiri Baraka, Haki Madhubuti, and Fay Chiang, all of us accompanied by Black Jazz as we overlooked those falls, I was struck by just how deep the American idiom really goes. Williams's *The Dog and the Fever* offers an intimate gaze into the workings of his mind, as he listened to what the Spanish satirists Espinosa and Francisco de Quevedo had in common with the experimental prose of Gertrude Stein and James Joyce in the early twentieth century. So, ladies and gents, get ready for a roller coaster of a ride in the pages to follow that will leave your head spinning.

— PAUL MARIANI —

Pedro Espinosa's novella *El perro y la calentura—The Dog and the Fever*—was originally published in Spain in 1625 during the height of the Golden Age of Spanish literature. It is a satire on court and church circles, and a minor classic among the great literary masterpieces of that so-called early modern period. As a poet and prose author, Espinosa (1578–1650) has been largely overshadowed by the giants of his day: Miguel de Cervantes, Lope de Vega, Luis de Góngora, and Francisco de Quevedo, to name the biggest. He and Quevedo were friends, according to some scholars. Espinosa compiled the celebrated 1605 anthology of contemporary poets, called *Las flores de poetas ilustres de España* (Flowers of Spain's Illustrious Poets), in which Quevedo's poetry first appeared in print. That was also the year of *Don Quixote*'s publication. A nobleman, politician, and sometime-exile from the royal court in Madrid, Quevedo became not only one of the most prominent poets of the early seventeenth century but a leading prose author and satirist, dubbed the Jonathan Swift of Spanish literature. The story of *The Dog and the Fever*, both the tale itself and the novella's long misattribution to Quevedo, puts him in the spotlight. Centuries after the book's debut, Quevedo through Espinosa and, at the same time, Espinosa through Quevedo captivated William Carlos Williams and his imagination.

Williams believed he was translating Quevedo, when in the fall of 1936, a few months after the start of the Spanish Civil War that deeply roused his personal Spanish identity, he set about to bring this novella into English with the help of his mother. She then was in her late eighties, bedridden, and living in his home. They accepted the stated authorship in their old edition of the book, published in 1736. Indeed, from the mid-seventeenth century until the mid-twentieth century, the author of the novella was generally considered to be Quevedo, who, according to the title page, "published it under the name of Pedro Espinosa."

The translation project was Williams's idea. He wanted to "amuse" his mother with it, as he had done to entertain his father with poetry translation during his final years, and also to use it as a subterfuge for extracting from her the story of her life growing up in Puerto Rico. She didn't want to talk about that. His "personal record" of her, *Yes, Mrs. Williams* (1959), was the ultimate result, parts of which appear in his introduction to the first edition of their translation of the novella that came out in 1954 from Shoe String Press.* But the translation itself became a

---

* Williams's friendship with Norman Holmes Pearson, an Americanist and literature professor at Yale, led to the publication of the novella by Shoe String Press, a now-defunct small press (1949–2004) that was located in Hamden, Connecticut. Pearson had asked Williams for a possible submission on behalf of the press, which was started as a private venture by two librarians at Yale. Williams took the opportunity to publish his translation, along with a new introductory essay.

work of extreme importance to Williams for a variety of reasons, not the least of which is the marked influence its baroque style of satire, its *conceptismo*, had on his composition of *Paterson*, which followed it in the mid-1940s.

When it came to translating Spanish, Williams always needed the help of an informant because his command of Spanish, though his first language as a boy growing up in Rutherford, New Jersey, "wasn't so hot," as he says in his *Autobiography*. In an early version of his introduction to *The Dog and the Fever*, he explains, "My mother, Raquel Hélène Rose Hoheb de Williams, . . . confined to her bed, did most of the work of translation." Of course, he is the one who completed the task and brought the meaning of the Spanish text that she gave him into well-crafted American speech, with his impeccable ear for the poetry of it. The manuscript of the translation went through multiple drafts—several of which include his mother's comments about individual words and phrases, together with the personal reminiscences they triggered of her childhood and early years. The first complete draft of their translation is dated May 23, 1944.

The Dog and the Fever led Williams to Quevedo's prose, at the New York Public Library, specifically to Charles Duff's collection of translations, titled *Quevedo: The Choice Humorous and Satirical Works* (1926). Williams spent a lot of time reading this anthology, plus Duff's biographical essay. He even translated the book's epigraph, taken from one of Quevedo's poems, which neatly demonstrates the style of *conceptismo* with the directness, everyday language, witty metaphor, and wordplay that attracted him to it: "I give you truths in chemises / (he said) / Not far from naked." Double entendre conveyed in a concise manner distinguishes this style, of which Quevedo is the most famous Castilian practitioner. Williams came to like Quevedo and his work so much that, in one of his handwritten notes that never found its way into print, he says, "Quevedo was a ~~great~~ good American"! This wild idea must be understood in the context of something Williams said publicly on more than one occasion: "In many ways sixteenth- and seventeenth-century Spain and Spaniards are nearer to us in the United States today than, perhaps, England ever was. . . . We in the United States are climatically as by latitude and weather much nearer Spain than England, as also in the volatility of our spirits, in racial mixture—much more like Gothic and Moorish Spain."

Quevedo dueled with Góngora in the literary controversy between *conceptismo* and *culteranismo*, also called *gongorismo*, since Góngora was its leading practitioner. *Culteranismo* is characterized by an ostentatious vocabulary, complex syntactic order, and overabundance of complicated metaphors. For Góngora, for instance, spring is "the flowering season of the year / when Europa's false-hearted abductor / —a half moon the weapons on his brow, / the Sun's rays all the strands of his hair— / oh bright glory of heaven, / grazes on stars in fields of sapphire blue; / when one who could pour the wine for Jupiter / better than the comely lad of Ida" (from *The Solitudes*, translated by Edith Grossman). The controversy was at times furious as a sword fight to the death, much like Williams's literary duels with T. S. Eliot over language and style. Williams also recognized that Wallace

Stevens was a modern American culteranist. In his 1937 review of Stevens's *The Man with the Blue Guitar*, he praised his poetry, but he also poked at his *culteranismo*, describing his language as "a language, God knows what it is! certainly nothing anybody alive today could ever recognize." Góngora's language could be described just the same way. Like Quevedo, Williams was after the more straightforward style, using direct spoken language.

In his introduction to the Shoe String edition of *The Dog and the Fever*, Williams opens with this comment about Quevedo, followed by the note about the origin of the translation:

> The difficulty with morals, as far as the artist is concerned, is that they tend to distract him from his labors in the arts. Anything that distracts the artist from his work or that forms a substitute for it or that rivals it in any way—a wife, politics, revenge, even the lures of fame—is for him immoral; and morals are among those defects.
>
> Had Quevedo retired to his country estate and devoted himself to the practice of writing, as his talents seemed to invite him to do, he would, we say, have been the greatest genius of Spain if not of the world in his time. But he was too impatient of his fate—tho' he did not marry until the age of 52. Stupidity, sycophancy, torpor infuriated him to such a pitch that he could not hold back, and his attack was direct and immediate. So alas were the repercussions: jail, wasting disease, and death, along with a small body of writing unworthy of so great a talent.

He was, to be sure, born to flourish, if he flourished, during a decadence of national prestige, a falling away immediately following the Golden Age of Spanish literature. . . .

When Mother and I began to translate *The Dog and the Fever*, I knew no more of Quevedo than the bawdy retorts reputed to him which had come down the two hundred years after his death even to Mayagüez [in Puerto Rico, where Williams's mother grew up] and so on to me. That's a rather long life for casual retorts, since the time of Shakespeare; many a man would be happy with far less fame. I'm sure Mother knew no more than I of the man, though it was his name which attracted us to the book which we finally took up and began to work on. It was something Ezra Pound had left in the house during one of his passages; I always wanted to know what the man meant by such a title, *The Dog and the Fever*. So we began to translate.

In his *Autobiography* Williams offers more of the backstory of the translation project, and there he says, "Someday I hope to make it attractive by doing a running commentary to accompany and interpret the text." The present edition does just that, to fulfill his desire at long last. I have added the commentary he wrote in the spring of 1949, which I found among his papers at Yale's Beinecke Library, placing it where he suggests it belongs and editing it slightly to adapt it to the present situation—now that we know the novella's true author, that is, the principal author.

The reason *The Dog and the Fever* was ascribed to Quevedo for so long is that the first edition of it was printed together with Quevedo's work, *Cartas del caballero de la Tenaza* (Letters of Sir Tightwad). Subsequently, as publishing was a very different, less controlled business back in the seventeenth century (despite the licensing of books), *The Dog and the Fever* was deemed to be a satire by Quevedo, included in collections of his work and also published as a separate volume under his name. That Quevedo was a "brand name" author whose books sold especially well was a factor too. A Spanish poet-historian, however, in the middle of the nineteenth century credited the novella to Espinosa, and later scholars supported his claim with additional proof. Despite that, even well into the twentieth century, the catalogs of many large collections continued to ascribe the work to Quevedo. Espinosa's use of a large chunk of Quevedo's own writing—pages taken nearly word for word from his famous "Sueño de la muerte" (Vision of Death)—further added to the confusion. In Espinosa's day, his immediate readers knew what he was doing with that intercalation, because they knew Quevedo. The long debate about the authorship finally ended with the definitive work of both Espinosa and Quevedo scholars in the latter half of the twentieth century.

Espinosa is an enigmatic figure in the history of Spanish literature. Details about his life are sketchy. The son of a family that was apparently middle-class, he was born and raised in southern Spain in the medieval town of Antequera, which in the early sixteenth century became known as "The Heart of Andalusia" because it was located at the crossroads of Málaga, Granada, Córdoba, and Seville. He is honored in his hometown as one of its great luminaries. Prosperous in his day, Antequera was a meeting place for important Renaissance writers and scholars. There a school of poets arose in which Espinosa became a leading member. He showed his prowess as a poet at an early age. Virtually all the major poets of the early sixteenth century are represented in his 1605 anthology of contemporary poets, which he compiled while in Antequera, attesting to his keen aesthetic judgment. His education included both theology and canon law, possibly in Seville, and also the literary arts in Antequera and then at the university in Granada, where he fell in love with a woman, a fellow student, who rejected him and, consequently, broke his heart. Soon after, he retreated to live in a hermitage outside of Antequera for a few years, changing his name to Pedro de Jesús. That led to his ordination as a priest around 1613–14—something a man without independent means might do to survive, or else become a civil servant to earn a living, among other things.

In 1618 Espinosa entered the service of the eighth Duke of Medina Sidonia, Juan Manuel Pérez de Guzmán y Silva—to whom he would dedicate *The Dog and the Fever*. That year Espinosa moved to Sanlúcar de Barrameda, a seaside town in the Cádiz province in Andalusia, where he spent the rest of his life. He was given the position of chaplain in the ducal household and also rector of San Ildefonso School, which trained poor children in Spanish and Latin letters. The duke was one of the outstanding literary patrons in Spain. Espinosa wrote the novella to amuse him, and it contains references to people and places in and around Sanlúcar, including the duke's garden and the milldam, which was not far from Espinosa's own house. The duke was a very rich nobleman, the son of the commander of the Spanish Armada. In fact, at the time his family was the most prominent wealthy family of the Andalusian region. While in his court, Espinosa benefited from his long support, both financial and literary.

The town of Antequera honored Espinosa in 1998 as a distinguished native son, erecting a large bronze statue of him standing with an open book in hand, in front of the Real Colegiata de Santa María la Mayor (Royal Collegiate Church of Saint Mary the Great), the first Renaissance church to be built in Andalusia. It was in this church that a grammar faculty was founded that gave rise to the Antequera school of poetry, which fostered Espinosa's career as a writer.

Espinosa modeled *The Dog and the Fever*, in part, on a quasi-picaresque novella by Cervantes titled *El coloquio de los perros* (*The Dialogue of the Dogs*), published in 1613 in a collection of twelve stories. Cervantes was the first to write novellas in Spanish—short stories in the Italian manner—both romance-based stories and realistic ones. *The Dialogue of the Dogs* may well be Cervantes's most profound and original creation, next to *Don Quixote*. Espinosa took the imaginary canine characterization a step further by disguising a public figure as a dog. Certainly, the talking dog, Chorumbo—the central character in Espinosa's novella—can be viewed as Quevedo himself. Espinosa's immediate audience must have laughed out loud at this portrayal of Quevedo. Williams was quick to perceive Chorumbo as a projection of Quevedo, who in 1620 had been driven from the court in Madrid and forced to live "in exile" for a time at his country place in Torre de Juan Abad, whose fiefdom his mother had purchased for him.

In an early draft of his once-planned introduction, Williams insists on the modernity of *The Dog and the Fever* and its image-driven narrative style: "There is a modern quality about it that is rather startling when the realization first strikes the eye, very much a literary collage, to tell directly a hidden story, if you will, without other explanation; almost a contemporary pastiche of words, proverbs, and phrases piled up often with very little reference to syntax. . . . Apart from a sort of atomic bombardment of words as words, each carrying its own unrelated particle contributing to the meaning (while remaining themselves uninflected—a nice point), the practice represented speed. And it is speed that characterizes our contemporary scene." He says the work "must be given a high place in ingenious literature." (The unpublished manuscript, which includes the statements quoted here as well as the running commentary on the novella, is available in the Williams section at wesleyan.edu/wespress /readerscompanions.)

The influence of the novella's satiric style—its rapid-fire *conceptismo*—on Williams's composition of his *Paterson* has yet to be fully appreciated. In Book I, put together in the mid-1940s when he was also finishing his translation and writing about *The Dog and the Fever*, Williams provided the satiric bedrock for his epic masterpiece. His later thought to credit Quevedo's "double entendre and bravura" in Books III and IV was based on his experience with the novella, for the early drafts of these books contained the lines: "At least these / are the words I prefer or / as Quevedo said: / like this you should never / write—and went on / from there." Indeed, the later books of *Paterson* include satiric elements presented through what he called "double talk": satiric jabs and parodic echoes that derive their force from baroque technique and accumulate meaning in accord with the foundation laid down in Book I. The many images of dogs in *Paterson* also connect it to the novella. As Williams told Horace Gregory, in describing the composition of Book IV, "dogs run all through the poem and will continue to do so from first to last. . . . Here the tail has tried to wag the dog." The most famous dog in the entire poem appears in the preface of Book I, and is the poet himself "sniffing the trees, / just another dog / among a lot of dogs."

Concerning the actual making of the translation here, Williams approached the task in much the same way he approached translating Spanish poetry—"using word of mouth and no literary English" (see his *By Word of Mouth: Poems from the Spanish, 1916–1959*). He aimed to bring the meaning of the Spanish text into the English spoken in the United States, what he famously called the American idiom. He was committed to using real speech with its distinctive rhythms and colorations. To add Golden Age Spanish flavor to the translation, he artfully seasoned it with occasional archaic language; he also included Spanish words, now and then, usually with his English rendering beside them. Overall, his efforts with his mother were aimed at finding accurate equivalents in English (paraphrase) and recreating the force of the original style. That force, he felt, was lost in the only other English translation of the novella, published in London in 1707 ("whoever did it didn't at all get the feeling," says Williams in his *Autobiography*).* That British translation is a domesticated version that strips the original of its foreignness and omits numerous passages, including the entire slang-heavy final pages. The Williams translation is decidedly more faithful than its eighteenth-century predecessor. Beyond that, it is a remarkable achievement in itself. It presents our poet's genius with American language, together with Espinosa's and Quevedo's dazzling *conceptismo*.

The fabled nitpicker Professor Horrendo, who can't see the forest for the trees, certainly could find occasional words and phrases at variance with the original Spanish. He would pounce on the translation of this passage, for example: "Perro soy. . . . Dios me libre de rabiar. . . . Y porque dije de rabia, no la habrá en el mundo hasta que haya Saludador." Williams rendered it this way: "I am a dog. . . . God save me from madness. . . . And since I speak of madness, there shall be none in the world till the Savior come." The literal meaning of the Spanish is "I am a

---

* John Stevens, the translator, "missed the entire point of the whole book, its double entendre" (William Carlos Williams to James Laughlin, 1944). See Stevens's translation in the Williams section at wesleyan.edu/wespress/readers companions.

dog. . . . God save me from getting rabies. . . . And since I speak of rabies, it shall not exist in the world till there is a Saludador." The fact is, a rabies-healer—*saludador* (now generally understood to mean quack doctor)—was an actual occupation that existed in early modern Spain, and Espinosa was not talking about Jesus Christ. The 1736 edition of the novella used by Williams, however, contains a typo and says "Salvador" (Savior), adding to his apparent mistranslation of *rabiar/rabia* and the rest of the passage. Specialists in early modern Spain might catch the textual error. Other editions, including the first, say "Saludador."

Faced with the faulty text, how was Williams—a far cry from a specialist in early modern Spain and its culture and language—to fully comprehend Espinosa here? Thus, his deviation from the strict literal meaning of Espinosa's actual Spanish. He did, though, achieve a perfectly reasonable rendering of the passage before him. It works. Rabies does cause madness in dogs (in fact, *madness* is an archaic term for rabies, which is the Latin word for it), and a rabies-healer could be a kind of savior, as the 1736 typesetter saw it. But all this is really beside the point: dictionaries don't make real translations. Williams succeeded in producing an essentially accurate translation of the novella as a whole, with its *conceptismo*'s fury of words. Ultimately, the translation is more about him and his own agenda in terms of his modernist experiment with language. The same is true of Williams's translations in general, both poetry and fiction, where occasionally he is inclined toward imitation to give them his personal stamp.

For help to finish translating the novella, Williams reached out in 1940 to Spanish poet Pedro Salinas, then teaching at Johns Hopkins, with questions about some of the unknown old words and slang in the original. "I confess mother and I were stumped by the four or five last pages, though they intrigued us immeasurably," he says in his commentary about it. He sent Salinas a letter, his first correspondence with him, also to thank him for a book of poems that Salinas had just published in translation. "But," as Williams later recounts, "he returned the script untouched, saying, 'This is written in early seventeenth-century slang, no one knows what it means now. Furthermore, the text is impure; the printers of those days made many mistakes. Some words, such for instance as *tablaoa*, are certainly not Spanish.'" Williams had to figure out himself how to deal with those challenging final pages, and he did, creatively.

The opening paragraph of that letter Williams sent to Salinas reveals much about himself and his attitude toward Spanish literature and our need to translate it: "In spite of my middle name I am not Spanish but more French and English than anything else. Yet, in another way I am very Spanish, due to childhood influences. I love the language and feel strongly for the Spanish tradition which is tremendously significant—and much neglected here. I think also that Spanish literature is a mine where we here in America might profitably dig for gold, the real gold of the world." Williams recognized *The Dog and the Fever* as a fabulous nugget of this literature. And here, of course, he himself shines with it.

—JONATHAN COHEN—

Dog and fever, what more natural to us?

We're dogs, all of us, at our best and worst if the fever

hasn't got us, all. Then let us find other means to hide it

than our present ones, for its sweat reeks from us. . . .

For a low-down mutt you've got to be low-down.

Low-down and double talk, to bring down the highest:

the Dog and the Fever.

—WILLIAM CARLOS WILLIAMS—

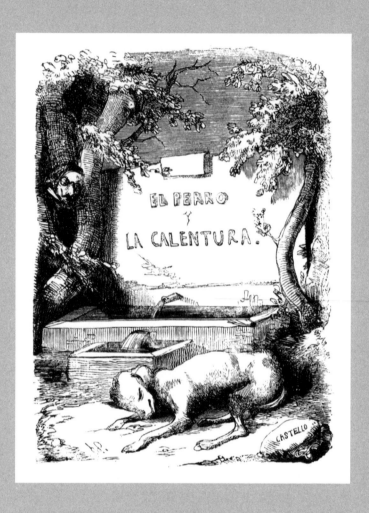

Let me, since the text is difficult, attempt to sum up briefly for the reader who may be interested the story of *El perro y la calentura*. It is gossip—with a sting—couched very much, generally, in the terms of the people.

The Dog (Quevedo) is so fed up with what he knows that he wants to shove in his fingers and disgorge the mess that is eating his heart out—but the author wishes, on a deeper level, to amuse, to amuse his patron and his patron's lady, who is his lectress: to bark, but not to bite!

He goes on, using the imagery of his surroundings, the country mill, the sayings of the people, "old Spain," in a sort of admiring contempt for them, facing what, of their own level, the corrupt court can laugh at, pitifully. The creatures of his fancy come from every corner, every peasant's hutch: the cat and the chestnuts. So he begins.

Gradually we find, as we read and the words begin to fly off apparently as unrelatedly as chips from a log being chopped—that a story is forming itself.

We catch glimpses of a theme—rushing toward some humiliation: the cuckold priest, the common girl who has betrayed him—and we look surreptitiously to the last pages—to a Moor? Nothing could be "lower"! And gaiety is increased in the world, and stupidity lessened, lessened in repute at least.

That's where the vulgar sayings of the people come in—he piles them up with evident gusto, both to reveal and to betray—portray how low his protagonist, the old boy, has got himself, into the hands of—is it the Prioress? a duenna with pietistic ways. But one knowing how to cut the cake seven ways for all that.

He is old, he is a greybeard, a beard dyed red—out of yearning for a youth long since lost. An old man who has been tricked into thinking he is still young—enough, and who keeps, injudiciously, a girl whom he has got with child, "all milk and honey," especially the milk.

"Look, girl," cautions the author, "you asked for it." And he goes on to tell what both must do and both must pay, out of mind and in fact—and there's to be no crying over it—piously as you may pretend otherwise.

To Don Fernando de Sotomayor,
who gave this discourse to be printed.

♠ So multiplex are my patron's interests that no one can have less claim upon Your Excellency, than he himself; and though through good works his powers increase, able as he is, he takes upon himself as much as man can do. It is as hopeless to present, as it is fruitless to imitate him, for in whatever it may be he outstrips us all. But compliments aside for the moment, though freely offered, of more worth it is, I affirm, to divert him from his lofty occupations (among others of the coach and garden) that I should write this Dog of good intention, vermin to enliven Your Excellency, of a disposition to sample vinegar, or in lusty vein, harassed by vulgar duties. Give ear to his Sibylline *pronunciamentos*, as mysteries, not as childish prattle; and pay heed in that (from the heat) the Fever speaks; cambric so fine, that from its periods, may be made up a collar of lace. Improve yourself

---

♠ *The prefatory letter to Sotomayor is not subtle in its flattery. But flattery was the game of the hour. In fact, they were too subtle to require that flattery pretend to be subtle. Let it go, broad and full. There's a dangerous charm in it, like present-day diplomacy.* [Editor's note: The 1736 edition of the novella—the source of the translation here—does not contain the dedication to the Duke of Medina Sidonia, for whom Espinosa wrote "this Dog"; see frontispiece, page ii.

(if you find reason) in these defects of others, for he who serves as a model is indeed worthless if you too do not see yourself in the speech of a boor and gossip. At the kindness which Your Excellency does me (even though it is more than I deserve) I discover no surprise, since each of us acts according to his nature and Your Excellency loves that which is his own. Commend me to our friends and procure for yourself health, and happiness, that I myself may have the same also.

Sanlúcar
October 15, 1625

The Dog and the Fever

*As I was strolling one evening by the milldam (Most Excellent Sir), I heard talking in a cane break. Opening a path, stork fashion, and listening with all the ears I had, I heard someone say: Madam Fever, I am a dog of the chase, a cynic court philosopher: my name is Chorumbo:[1] my liver is petrified by grievances, upon the tip of my tongue I carry a thousand secrets: I long to shove in my fingers and loosen the hooks of my breast. Your Ladyship has come pat to my purpose: no one overhears us, keep my course as you hope to be knighted, I will no more than hint at griev-

---

We find at the start what passes for a crystal brook! But unhappily there are no crystal brooks in the world today. And "God deliver us from virtuous men, lodged in easy places, who do no more than drink and talk. They are without conscience but, like pigs who have gorged themselves, still continue to root and grunt."

The Bishop—a simonist and pious cuckold—follows rapidly under the eye of the satirist. Money and women. But especially an old man on a colt.

"I speak of caballeros," that is the gentry. "But what a penurious clutch they are. Pretentious. Without equipage and besotten."

Ah, the girl is barely fifteen, poor, and urged on by her mother or Mother Superior to take the old guy over. "Well, if you must," says our author, "do it whole hog. Don't wear gloves if you have decided to go it naked."

"Very often by trusting the dog," etc. Who could that be, the duenna? "The wolf sleeps in the straw." There is danger ahead. Gossips are already at work and Papa had better watch his step.

"Do I make myself clear?" The word is out; everybody knows what is going on and he's going to be taken and taken proper before he is through.

ances. I took a fairer stand to listen, and he continued by saying: Clowning, clowning, the wolf devours the ass. Does anyone hear us? I talk low, go down a peg, like one who closes a door, for the pot boils over. One eye to the gridiron and another on the cat; and that we may begin at the source: Do you not see, Your Excellency, this small trickle, that looks so clear and pleasant, that laughs with all things, and chatters of everything, seeming more a creature of the Palace, than urines of the mill? God deliver me from virtuous men for whatever accursed purpose, lodged safely in sinecures, to drink and to talk. Conscience scorches them, to no avail; they cut the finger for the turnip. Tongues longer than their hands, wry mouths, that slash as with dull scissors. Pigs, that even after they have gorged themselves continue quarrelsome and grunt. God destroy lying tongues, that even send up praise to Judas, with octaves, and excuse him, saying, that he was so hungry, he shook the grain from ears of wheat, and that begging alms of God, they gave him no more than a rope; and that the poor Bishop seeing himself involved in simony, and condemned to suspension, it wasn't much to put on the face of a hanged man, and signal with the tongue as at cards, to make you hate a pious cuckold. The soup was lost between the hand and the mouth: pass on to other things. My Lady, he who has no goats, how shall he sell kids? Honey in the mouth, do you perchance relax guard over the purse? Is the billy more honest because he wears a beard? Does the mallet cut by being of iron? To fight for rye bread, is it not evidence of great hunger or slight friendship? The guitar tells it: Sweet the death of your mother-in-law, sure shot with a rolling-pin: dangerous to play ungloved with a cat: to play the fool with women, or money: sow thistles, and walk barefoot. Stitch this mouth from corner to corner; but first permit me two words: Believe me, Your Excellency, that that which fleas are to a dog, rats to cheese, women, and devils, the same is an old man on a colt, that is to say, one devil on another. I speak of caballeros, that because the servants ask for no cheese, they give them no bread. Those that have more ancestors, than particles in a pork hash: more blood than a sausage, sugar wits and for that reason good for desserts, that (leaving the mind aside) are so much the more so many peafowl. Tassels, balls of raff, skeins of silk, more a matter of horses than of horsemen; that play with words as with lances; know letters as they do the Christian dogma: the intelligence of images, who after saying: It's a fine day (in order to say something) have nothing more to say, and their speech rises to the ceiling, so much so that it can't be fetched down again with a candlelighter. They are the debtors: that lie, and write askew: they wear spurs without having a horse, and peacock about in rented livery; but no one can at the same time swallow and blow; but look of whom I am thinking: Girl of fifteen, who hopes for a worthy husband, pheasants, or fast: can't you see, that time stretches out, breasts also, and the table calls for more than a clean cloth? Sister, look, it is absurd to be naked and wear gloves: if you wish to carry rye, make of yourself a packsaddle; and if you desire to be kissed on the breast, make a melon of yourself. To go on: Very often by trusting the dog, the wolf sleeps in the straw. Do I make myself clear? Let jail and Lent be for the poor; let the sparrows quarrel over somebody else's wheat; let the big pot make a small will; let someone else go for the salt pork and come back lacking ears; let excessive courtesies be a sort of deception; threaten with a gun and wound with the sword; stroke with one hand and stab with the other; that before the door of the other, there be a pit, and a whistle, to fall in, and to blow; that there is no virtue lost nor head broken without an uproar; ♠ that the cat be Don Gonzalo,[2] no more than by being a cat, and if you falsify the midwife's records, how will the case be improved? It's like pounding water in a mortar. Pity on you, wicked world, poorly muffled! Who shall follow all your crazy zigzags? Who shall ordain you with such silly rites? You have paid the hire of the bells, to lead the dance of the jailed. Although you are gay as a pig going to the

---

♠ *"That the cat be Don Gonzalo." "Pity on you, wicked world, poorly muffled!" "Who shall follow all your crazy zigzags?" But he will not be thrown off the scent by such maneuvers.*

The old man, with a beard dyed three colors, begins to act kittenish. There are castanets and tambourines lively to his mood.

But the Dog, feeling he is pressing malice too close, halts his ridicule. "After all, all truths are not to be spoken" [as Quevedo says in his Sueños (Visions)]. And, after all, you should not complain, you're lucky to have the privileges of a husband and had better say thank you and call it quits. It might be worse—and probably is. Don't boast about it. There are many things you should be grateful for.

Now follows a list of a fool's perquisites, at which "he" should not be surprised—since they affect him so closely—if he only knew!

fair; tree without fruit, I pronounce you kindling. Who would not cross himself before you, as before La Bermuda?[3] O, old man, face like the spout of a jug, nose like a hoe, have you no shame to throw gherkins at the truth? Shall sheepskin beard be heralded by castanets and merry looks? The brain lies not in the beard. You, that should be more harnessed than a mill mule, or duenna on a visit, and speak with the belly's mouth, like a fat archdeacon, do you pluck the lute, clash timbrels, and shake the tambourine? But hard upon malice, an end to that. It seems to me, that a wish to be easy would suffice, saying: Dog, that pisses on doorsteps, what white poll do you comb, what purple robe is this in which to canonize? Don't bring the evangelical scruples of an old piety affecting woman into vulgar affairs; don't let other lives be your death. Can't you see, that misfortunes are sought out like money? Your eyes are clearer than an envious neighbor's. All truths are not to be spoken.

> To call themselves fairly beaten,
> Husbands themselves thieves and cuckolds,
> Though they speak only the truth
> Press a point ill taken.

You complain of shortage of bread and many children; a full stomach may well fast: Don't tie Time with a friar's girdle; much easier to suffer it than to reform it. Your studies are Thomistic, for they stop with questions. Don't make carrion of him, for tomorrow will be Judgment Day: but if in spite of all, the flail of your currish state continues to beat,* don't be surprised at that, rather at the privileges of a husband. At the honeyed drivelings of a Mother Superior. At the mincings of a fop. By my mother's soul, at the musket shots of a Galeno. At the drunken thwackings of a bailiff. At the dry concepts of dogma. At the bull of the nativity that dare not say this mouth is my own. At the staff of justice not worth an egg. At a prior, keg and belly. At a bride, pinecones, and wine in the name of Juan Barbón.[4] At a young girl, guitarred, not to say violated. At the five holy orders, like a falcon. At a judge stunned, by a deceitful blow, the blow of a great cat. At a clerk of the court, who speaks of the present, old man yesterday, and Jew to come. At there being no Moors, and gossip aplenty. At

---

*This is one of the author's "lists," put down without comment other than the facts of which they speak. This in itself is a fascinating sort of composition, used several times in this work—almost contemporary in its literary method: no comment, nothing "about" the subject, a bare placing of the matter before the attention, as an object, that which with wit a man might see for himself, swiftly and to the point. The list is loaded with the author's contempt. The ridiculousness of a "blacksmith in a damask apron."

Much else might be said, but, addressing his reader, the Dog calls a halt in his indictment. Or does he? It is only a pause in which to get his breath before barking more loudly than ever. For on he goes lashing out with ridicule at "a child" (infant) of sixty years who already says "Daddy." "Look, old man, wine is good—but no more than four shots at the most. Be warned and—take it easy. I tell you this out of the goodness of my heart!"

Then back comes our author to his original figure of the reeds that surround the mill. "I mean no evil, really," he says. "I am a dog; to bark, not to bite." Ha! But "God save me from madness."

And "Suddenly I betook myself to the garden, with my doggish speech, short as the luck of a greybeard, verse of a dirge, or hair of goat. Pardon me, Your Grace, that I think to cool the soup by barking; and thus coming back to my thema, or anathema, I would ask, lady mine: For whom does the blind man's wife adorn herself?"

And there we are again.

an old woman, who shrugs her shoulders. At pestles of glass. At a widow, who in the fool's confession, petitions the church. At that the best friend has still two small fingers' worth of Iscariot in him. At a hermit at court. At Saint Zulema. At not permitting the altar boy to swallow his spit. At the friendship of a mother-in-law. At poultice of male flattery, that reeks nine months of what's to come. At deceit, in a flowing dress. At being ill of secrets, and cured by vomiting. At the soul of a thief, well water not to be reached lacking a rope. At a lean funeral of small cost. At full pelt, that it takes strength to lift the wineskin. At earth, that yields better turnips, than letters. At woman, dog-like, that never runs alone. At vague thinking. At diarrhea of phrase, as though from leaves of Laurencio Vala.[5] At stubbornness, that consents out of the love of God. At practicing the cornet where there is no echo. At buttering of the plea, for it to come of itself, that a favorable verdict fall into open purse. At damsel, with a bill for milk, to sooth the nipples of her breasts. At being called, and to testify, like a witness to a will. And at a blacksmith in a damask apron.

My friend, you are right; but for that reason I must applaud other evils with Pythagorean silence, and smooth the way for the reader, saying: Make way, let the swill pass. Why should I not be amazed, if Homer nods? I must bark if I see the branch at the door, and the frail at home. I'm not so simple as to send the wolf for meat, nor drink myself full at mealtime, for though I singe not my wings, neither do I wet them. I have my share of bitterness, my intrigues, and loyalties. Tell me then, what climbing place shall we give to a child of sixty, who already says

Daddy; better to be drunk than anointed for death, and sweat more than cough. I am a toper, let God's will be done. Padre, consult your pillow, flee like a cat from the blacksmith's sparks, from the breath of the tankard, although you have something of Barbarroja[6] about you. Don't stop putting water in your wine just because there are creeping things in the river. Look, old man, wine is good; if it is good, I give you leave, and to the crusty wise wig also, that you may exceed three, but not four, shots. To raise the thirst with salt fish shall not be permitted to Tiberio. Why treat of ships, since you have not seen water, nor today, hand's breadth of earth, transformed in Christ's first miracle?

I say not a word that in tropologic sense has not more mysteries than letters, and I fear lest these reeds shall not turn to flutes and give it out that Midas pricks his ears. But we die of fear that these words should fall into the wolf's ears. I am a dog; to bark, not to bite: God save me from madness, for today there is no more to do than kill fleas with the teeth; and since I speak of madness, there shall be none in the world till the Savior come; nor possessed of the devil, till there be Cleric to conjure them. It is not wise to cross a wooden bridge on horseback; enough to sprinkle it with a goat's beard. He praised writing with a peacock plume, because it has eyes. Suddenly I betook myself to the garden, with my doggish speech, short as the luck of a greybeard, verse of a dirge, or hair of goat. Pardon me, Your Grace, that I think to cool the soup by barking, and thus coming back to my thema, or anathema, I would ask, lady mine: For whom does the blind man's wife adorn herself? Why does the Father Preacher of the *Flos Sanctorum* sell us flour in the cup, that he took from

Ruth's ears of corn, in the stubble fields of Valderrama? Why must the hen crow before the rooster? What good is patience if when we have need of it we don't find it? Why must I drag my sturdy legs about till it seems they are being pulled off me? Why must they make entry of the saints in the Almanac de Juan Redondo in red letters? Why should he blush who has no shame at home? ♠ And the Mother Prioress, why does she not spend each day gazing upon a pound of eyes? And thou (brimming over with

---

♠ *Now comes the Mother Prioress—who must have been in on the scheme. But "beware of silence, lest a belch at vanity should cause the most austere of hermits (Quevedo?) [Espinosa?] to burst into laughter."*

And alas, alas and alas! We begin again one of the lists that make this writing what it is: a literary device of charm and puzzlement—a definite invention for our amusement and a veiled instruction.

"For what does the moon care that the dog bays her"—nor a young wife for her old husband? "Alas, that he who puts foot in a brothel, puts another in the hospital!" And so on for two more pages. Followed almost at once by a second catalog in the same vein upon the themes of "All" and "Every" and then, "Don'ts," "Do nots," and "Believe." This is our satirist in his ribbing mood, tongue in cheek, the "writer" writing for the fun of it.

"Believe me, Christian people, that no cuckold is lost for lack of a bellwether." And, "Don't believe in an old man redyed, with the recipe of the flamingo, who making himself son of himself, and blotting out with logwood"—poor old bugger—"the brushstrokes of God, changes his marks like a donkey stolen by a gypsy."

And "Grey-haired fool, because you put your trust in a duenna, etc. etc. etc." "Protect the girl." Then to the girl, "Child, sell yourself dear, which is to say, well loved."

He ridicules the fashion-mongers of his day who speak too prettily, "smoke of green gourds," and again a catalog and God protect us from evil, from this, from that, "from the searching eyes of neighbors," etc., etc. for a page and more. All manner of admonitions toward correct conduct, advice to policemen, druggists, Father Confessors, and many more.

On page 26, in a short verse, he admonishes us to "pay heed to these concepts," for under the load (the packsaddle) lie hid many secrets for us to decipher—if we can.

offences, sufficient to make thee stuff thy face full of fingers), by that which thou complainest of the mule and the Padre, I say it is the truth that San Francisco went afoot, for in that time there were not so many beasts of burden as there are now. Beware of silence, lest a belch of vanity should cause the most austere of hermits to burst into laughter. Alas, how unsafe it is to lend money the wrong way, nor good to receive with one measure and dispense with another! Alas, that the rats make no game of the cat's son! Alas, that who at twenty-one is not, at thirty knows not, at forty has not, never will he be, know, or have! Alas, that he who sleeps may not fish! Alas, that to eat with borrowed money is to pay with your own! Alas, that he who puts foot in the house of a prostitute puts another in the hospital! I wept, since that same organ which serves for seeing serves also for tears. But what does the moon care that the dog bays her? But since there is no old man lacking his complaints, and hunger brings the wolves from the forest, I return to my lamentation. Alas, that the marriage year is debt or sickness! Alas, that the crow weeps over the sheep, and the next day eats it! Alas, that evils and mushrooms are not born single! Alas, that woman finds no more of what she is after, and in this there is no difference among women! She who loves, or is loved, leaves the purse empty: this, if she be beautiful, is not wholly her husband's: this is the old man's enemy; this is the life and death of her home; and to tell the truth, merchandise is deceiving—wine, horses, and women. He who has he-goats has horns: he who has but one son, he drives him crazy: he who has one pig alone, it deafens him: he who has to do with honey licks his fingers; and he who eats salad will not go to bed fasting. Alas, that the old man who weds suffers the malady of a kid, which soon dies, or comes to be a grown buck; his whole body is spent, and the head grows! Alas, that good she-goat, good she-mule, and good duenna are three evil beasts! Alas, that woman and wine deceive the most sagacious! Alas, that woman, servant, doctor, cat, and the scrivener are five necessary evils! Alas, that woman and she-goat, if she be lean, can outeat Judas! Alas, that it is not possible to put faith in a beard of three colors! Alas, that the most secret is nearest to being secret! Alas, that he who trusts no one is silly, and he who trusts everyone is crazy! Alas, that he who has a cough, love, or a woman who affects discretion lacks no other evil, but he who has little cloth will be short of habit! Alas, that the fasting Padre abstains from sparrow hawk when he might eat young partridge! Alas, that the bull should beg leave of the one presented, but why does the lamb seek greetings of the wolf? Alas, what does the cat care for the threats of rats, and that there be no lack of ailments for him who would kill his own dog! Alas, madam woman, he who whitewashes his house has it for rent, but he who rents expects damages! Alas, good man, that he who makes more to do about you than usual wants to cheat you, and he who tastes green fruit repents of it, making wry faces! Alas, that living without sorrows is not easy for mortals and that in a dotard there is nothing firm! Alas, that the earth gives all things, and receives all things, and all that time makes, he unmakes! Alas, how hard it is to choose melons, for a duenna to be a saint, bed a greyhound, and guess right in marrying! Alas, my friend, don't praise yourself; don't think ill of the good; nor choose a woman by candlelight, nor goods either; don't wish to know what is boiling in my pot; don't choose a friend at a banquet; you should not trust yourself more than you trust others, nor trust the serenity of the sea, nor of woman: believe me, that there is no rose without thorns, nor goat dead of hunger. You understand me now. Not all learned men are wise. All haste brings its own slowness. Time discovers all things. Everything wants its right measure. All cuckolds have two against one. Every mill demands its water. All excess is vicious. Everyone looks for his profit. All praise that which is their own. Everyone has his faults. He that does villainies is himself vile. Everyone loves so that others may love him. All bread of your neighbor is sweetest. All that which is feared is distrusted. All work has its price. All prodigality is not generosity. Money buys everything. A great thirst cannot be put out of mind. Every ill destroys or is destroyed. All small pots make large purses and all repentments cost dear. Brother, rather one eye than blind, rather rule than rent, rather security than bail. Tie so that you may untie. Don't drink what you can't see. Don't deal lightly with the truth. Don't ask grapes of the hawthorn, nor praise until you have tasted. Pay, and you will know that which is yours. Don't cheat where you will be found out. Give me advancement, the more if you don't love me. Do for me, I'll do for you. Teach yourself first, before those you love well. Blow, and you will not burn yourself. Choose for yourself fish of three years, wine of two, meat of one, bread of yesterday, egg of today, the cheese that weeps, and broth with a hundred eyes. Little of Venus, few words, few cares, and less to eat, and mild, that the soup has seven virtues. Takes away hunger, quenches thirst, sweetens the belly, cleans the gums, brings sleep, eases birth, and brings two roses to the cheeks. Believe me, no breed of dogs, love of a whore, laborer's riches, or silver kept in a pitcher lasts more than three years. Do not lend, for if it were good to lend, woman would lend herself. By virtue of three things you will be rich—earn and do not spend: promise and do not keep your promise, receive and fail to return: and notice that there are five things that thrive most in the world and consume you most—cheating, the itch, the goat, chilblains, and woman. He who has ears, listen. God deliver me from small eyes and from meddling where staves are in action, from giving a banquet, for he who has to spend for it does not enjoy it; from building a house, because it must be large, or small, or high, or low. Keep moving, hare, monk, student, and let the prostitute be close to the street. I will say for the others, that having a soul nearly as black as a tailor, she is very sure of her salvation, by lighting each night a lamp to our Lady of the Underworld, and that a blind man pray the orison of the Just Judge. I have the tongue of a cat, that even by licking draws blood.

Several nuns of Granada, having finished chanting the vespers to Saint John, many people being in the church, there went up into the pulpit Doctor Sumo Campo[7] (and I being present) he began to preach, saying: San Juan, San Juan more thought of than loaves of gold and the Jewish Sabbath, if you grant me grace, I will give you a good day: today that you are more sung than bread and wine for All Saints, it has not been necessary to give notice of my sermon—so as not to ring bells for carrot salad. But since cash is not growing in the bag, and the big purse is for occasion only, I say that I have much contraband put away in the storehouse of silence, but this time their very bowels shall be loosened, in that I kill being mum, if I frighten by speaking; and so, Ladies Mothers, I must say it, even to the stupid and addle-brained, even though (in the manner of today's saint) preached in the desert, whose head they cut off, the truth, through a wh . . . (I was going to say it) and must have been since she showed the lamb to the wolves. Believe me, Christian people, that no cuckold is lost because of a bellwether. Don't believe in an old man redyed, with the recipe of the flamingo, who making himself son of himself, and blotting out with logwood the brush-strokes of God, changes his marks like a donkey stolen by a gypsy who says: I have a bridle, that I may not want for a hack. Don't trust gypsies, Aprils, or fine gentlemen, for all are full of promises. The world is lost, those that enter young bachelors come out son-in-laws. With three visits, pregnant upon one head: It is wise to visit the goodwoman but not every day. A hard thing to keep people at home. Opportunities and dangers are all one. Simple; do you put wooden pots on the fire? He who would fetch others to his own hermit makes a miracle monger of himself; and to create many out of one, says: Jock, Jack, and John and all is one (*oliva, olivo, y azeytuno, y todo es uno*);[8] for add up duck, goose, and gander, it sounds like four things, and is one. There is no fool who does not die in harness. How many condemn themselves simply by being fools? There is no other kindling in hell. By fools the world is sustained, for in each house at least one is required (*Porro unum est necessarium*);[9] and every fool yields his folly, though we be never so much a toper to need of pestle to roll down twenty steps. But sad to say, we are not wise to it, and while we go stumbling, we content ourselves by saying: Everything tumbles down at home. Grey-haired fool, because you put your trust in a duenna, who prays the service of the dead, because your honor is lost, be careful lest these coifs and fine Holland stuffs fall not over long sleeves upon those for whom not even the Portal of Saint Mary is uncertain. Protect the girl (most reverend chin whiskers) don't give the duenna a master; see how they are talking apart; and walk as close together as flame and candle, zipi, zape, Vespers and Compline. Flanders is no more in Guinea than to hear how an old woman instructs a young girl graduate. Child, prudence is to think many things, and do one, and chiefly to deceive many, and think of not one. Sell yourself very dear, which is to say, well loved. Don't let a day pass without a line. To the tepid put fire. If you don't want the pot to be burned at the fire, stir it; if it boil up add a little cold water; if you wish it to boil, poke up the fire, because for tough meat, bellows, hot coals, and go to it. That which I can assure you is, that none will fail to be cooked by fault of a lid. Make it a high portal for the reputations of those who enter, and black as a crow for those who leave. Thrust in your fists, and you will have good dough. To the old female tanner of gloves, what worth the knob of the parchment roll of bulls; there I have the satchel of my sermons, if you need paper. Who will be able to suffer a gentleman jackass, official grafted upon a count, whose father was drowned in an oil bottle, that the very devils cannot bring peace to the fury of his slapstick, and with buttons overhauled, his smock ironed, and in the very finest coat of Venice, for a sixth of gold that he carries in his little hat, says: By my faith of a caballero (but he should say of a horse) the bay has a pretty mouth, and halts on his feet; well, thickhead, on what else then shall he come to a halt? Why such airs, that come to your mouth, if not to tell the torment of your noodle? Thus do towers bend, when muleteers would ascend them that are to be found at their feet, and you are so tall because you climbed on a bale of goods to reach knighthood, like a grapevine. Knight, *cañarí*,[10] smoke of green gourds, behold your nose makes more of a show than your knighthood. I know that you must rise against me, since it is not fitting that you should hear the gospel sitting down. It is as great nonsense to ask for the iron mines of Viscaya,[11] merely to come by a hemstitch needle, as for him who would kill a pig to inquire as to the cleanliness of its grandparents and to look at the teeth of a gift horse. And the same to sanctify the Blessed Mother, who says with tears and self abuse: Blessed be the soul's spouse, and because she is overjoyed in that the Mother of the Twenty-Four[12] is come to visit her, and by right of holiness, wishes not to spin, for it is no mark of death that he has a crooked tail, nor neck of a goose, the badge of suffering and meekness. Also he who speaks of serious things stuttering, like a Berber, or jug that is emptying, and with thumbs in his belt swells up like hot bread soup. Foolish the abbot who struggles all his life, if at last he must die of the cold. Father, did God give you no children and did the devil give you nephews? You are bright like the key to a portal and fat as a Carthusian pig. By Saint Martin, I will wait for you, that you may give the best day to your people. One shall catch the blood of your regal veins, another carry away the pieces, and you will remain clean, without feet or head. It happened to me getting up at night to study, meaning to take up a candle, I grasped instead a piece of sausage, and going to put the bellows to the fire where the cat was lying, his eyes were ablaze, and as the sausage approached him, he sank his teeth into it, and ran off with it, leaving me bewildered and without having studied. By his warning eyes, the cat is a devil; see, that in taking up the candle, you don't grasp some knave of a Prosecutor who helps his client (resigned to die in good faith) and a clerk of the court, with claws already grasping. Luckless the litigant, who buying the rope with his own cash, thinks to put the fool to rest. So during Carnival at Barcelona let you be merry, who tomorrow will become ashes, for in order to fry the eggs they are looking already for the pan. But quitting the company of goats and black clawed ravens, I say, may God deliver you from complying with the church for mere compliance sake, because it will be mere compliance. From making the doctor your heir. From sparrows that fly up before everyone equally. From abbot turned clergyman, to whom for myself I should not trust my own mother. God save you from other favors of a hidalgo with a lamp in the entry, at the cost of oil from his own salad, that kills his hunger with letters patent of nobility; from a good market of Roman noses; from Pope's mouth, and the eye of a cardinal; from inviting the Jew (if he be your uncle) for Mass or salt pork, because fleeing Saint Anthony's pig, he will fall into Saint Anthony's fire; from him who chases after woman and comes away with woman troubles; from drinking before thinking; and from him who wants to be thanked, that throws acorns to pigs; from a gentle drip that wears away stones; and from castration, when you quarrel with your wife; from the searching eyes of neighbors; from vineyard near the highway; from talkative woman, and fire near flax; from beard in which the official mediates; from taking a candle into the wind; from egg, and tow; from the more complaining than in pain; from shoes put on backward, that they may not follow in his tracks; from foster mother that eats; from a shop owner; from haft that weighs more than the maul; from *blanca y cornado*;[13] from an old woman, of whom the wrinkles say they are from the torments of jealousy you cause her; from resin plasters by which to enjoy the cheapness of a headache; from squanderer without means, for it would have to be either a miracle, or a thief; from pious (appearing) man putting on with heavy apostolic boots, and the neck of a flute, with rosary in hand, and the Alkoran[14] in his breast; from friendship of son-in-law; from the winter sun; from a spoonful of soft bread, and from flowers made of horn; from her who talks with the devil and is frightened by a mouse; from poppied donkey; from judge's staff, that bends double from bearing the weight upon one end; and to walk and walk and get nowhere. O corrupt world, were you not round you would be tall and skinny; I don't know how to remedy you. During the passing of the storm, praised be Jesus Christ of the pilgrimage. There is nothing more certain at a banquet, than haste, bad manners, and a drunkard. Know, my friends, that if the marksman is poor, there is no safer spot for you than at the target. The illness of another is

Galen's gain.[15] Dull students end by becoming druggists. To lend to your enemy is to win him, and to a friend, to lose him. All things come in their time, brands in February, horns in absence, and turnips at Advent. It is a good way to rid himself of the visitor for the sick to ask for the pot. He who cannot laugh, let him think of the old woman with a bun, or tickle himself. He who cannot weep, let him get a mother-in-law or cut up onions. Don't wear a cap at a banquet. Your manners be without manner. Don't put an embroidered saddlecloth on an old donkey. And in order that the ass does not wander off, it's a hard thing that the doctor comes before science. Man, the best walking is a good mule, good purse, and to remain at home. Enamor yourself of the church, letters, the sea, of the Royal Palace, of well chewed and well wetted. And believe, honest and true, that there is no first without a third, nor palm that gives fruit lacking a hand to cultivate it. If you desire a pleasant moment, drink cold. Good hour, eat at home. Good day, shave your beard. Good week, kill a pig. Good month, bathe. Good year, marry. And if you wish a good life, keep a good conscience. Fall in love with bread of Segovia; water from the Sierras; shade of a roof; with priest's stew, who swallows soup like an awkward pup. Believe me, that there is no perfection in having an ell and a half of neck. Don't trust in patience offended. Have the eye of a falcon, ears of an ass, sense of smell of a she-donkey, mouth of a shoat, back of a camel, and the legs of a deer; and don't wish to judge everything you see, believe everything you hear, do everything you can, say all you know, keep everything you have, spend all you possess.

For the persistent beggar, have great dispatch. Beware of Pero Ganso,[16] that as you find her, so you take her. He to whom you wish ill, eat his bread, and to whom well, the same: if there is little, begin first. I want no young woman to play upon me unless she knows how to spice the stew and put a sole in my other sock. Confessor, who visits young girls, from this moment I mark you for *pater familias.*[17] Policeman, put on a cape, lest they piss on you. Druggist, carry a pack of cards, that you may play many games with them. Master, you do not keep your servant for love, but for what you get out of him. Therefore, your servant does not follow you but your money.

> Pay heed to these concepts
> For under the packsaddle ride secrets.
> God's Grace and Glory.

* The Fever replied: Glorified am I to behold Your Grace so zealous for the profit of souls. I came to drink, lying upon my face, from these coursing crystals; and to make my home in the

---

* *At last, the Fever begins her story. Going back to the first scene, she says in effect, "I came to drink, lying on my face, from these coursing crystals—but, edified as I find myself to be at your discourse, I prefer brevity."*

"I have traveled, I have seen this, I have seen that." But before long the Dog resumes and on we go: proverbs: "Don't pull so hard that it breaks," "Measure yourself with your own rod," always directed to the game in question—for six pages: "Stains come out by rubbing," etc., etc., until we arrive at "the doctors." Sound and sage advice to whoever will profit by it—that old man keeping a young girl for his pleasure—might well profit by.

For now the doctors come! Now Quevedo [himself] lets go. It is a favorite figure in Italian and earlier stories, but the point is not dulled in Quevedo's telling. "But inasmuch as neither friends nor enemies are good witnesses, let us change the subject."

peach-laden branches of your office, both I have forgot, harking to pronouncements so clipped, combed, and laconic that it is enough for the sausage merely to have seen the fire. I crave brevity, I am drugged to death. I lean to Seneca, good lime, and sand, which is to cement stones with gold. But let Lope de Vega say what he will at the Fair, there is only one in the world to gongorize.[18] Permit me the *Antidote* and school of Señor Herrera. I ask a razor-thin slice. Don't slit my throat with a bran shovel, I can't bear a wide prairie, still less Lilibeo.[19]

I have traveled and seen so much, that I can well come to the aid of Your Grace with confirmation, no guesses, which would be no more than to smear with mud, but seen with these eyes: pardon me the pleonasm. From me the Turk defends himself by going about, the Moor fasting, the German drinking, the Englishman swallowing, the Flamande vomiting, the Spaniard bleeding, the Indian dancing, the Italian sleeping, and the Frenchman purging off, from which there have followed, to witness, more evils than those bewept by Your Grace; but he who attends expects it, since bitter mouth will spit no sweet. If this be not so, let my miserable condition turn it sour, as that of Your Grace barks upon it. Today I was annoyed hearing two gracious stay-at-homes, quarreling over points of honor, and he: You a lady, and I gentleman, who shall saddle the mule? I feel often ashamed out of anger, seeing the world fuller of excellences than mercies, accustomed in their breasts to doing no good. He who swears by my conscience, I look at once at his hands. The most disastrous to houses I find to be woman, smoke, the cat, and the kettle, and that many evils are contained in one: in woman, in the hospital, a bullet, in jail, and the innkeeper. The toga of the man of letters cloaks the persistence of the litigant. The madman trusts his wife to another, permits others to try his sword and to count his money; and to revenge himself on the rats, burns down his own house, though it is truth that there is no pantry without them. I notice that there is lack of friendship but not of friends; that the blind have mirrors, idiots lecterns. Sardine is bait for trout, and I have seen no mother-in-law that was welcome. In heredities I find a little of all things: science without brains is insanity, and that the dog fawns for his bread. He who would live in this world, give heed, and do not fret: pay, and you will have riches: gold, that they may swallow: scratch each one where it itches him: keep your purse and your mouth closed. Measure yourself with your own rod. Don't feel yourself secure in privations. Don't pull so hard that it breaks. Don't try to accomplish more than you can do. Don't worry other ears. Teach yourself first. Think many things and do one, and have your man in every doorway. Know, that every scale has its counterweight, and that word of honor is worth much and costs little: that patience, time, and money succeed in all things; and that to seem, without being, is warp without woof; and that time, words, and stones return never to the hand. He who would live to be old, let him fear only God. Dress warmly, eat moderately, for to pleasure we owe little and much to health. Don't go seeking breath that no others have breathed. Grasp the eel with leaves of the fig. Give the shoe that pinches to your servant, content yourself with little. Limit your expectations, for death comes wrapped in hopes, and a gold ring will not cure a stye, nor crown a headache; but this is a great hardship of life, that the windmill has no need to be screeching and cannot turn without it.

All moves as God orders. That is, to go to banquets, rather than to a health resort. Money is the herb to cure all the ills of woman. Luck reaches further than long arms. Ill fortune outruns a lampoon making the rounds. The same that yesterday was a buck is today leather. To a hundred of rent, a thousand for vanity, and the estate will come to an end before the folly. No one measures himself with his own rod. Vexations are drowned in cups. Embroiderers and packsaddle makers, they say, both ply needles. And packsaddle makers dub themselves doublet makers in the rough. Writers, secretaries; butchers, carvers; slaughterers, butchers; and the gambling house, the house of assignation; harlots, courtesans; and the hangmen, doctors. Asses die, and they bury wolves. We pardon those in trade, for that of which they have not robbed us. The hope of pardon makes crimes easy. A lance of gold kills all you may desire. Interest puts an end to friendship. Fruit near the highway does not ripen. The married quarrel by day but at night sleep with their buttocks together, heads apart like the Imperial Eagle. The pleasure of that which you own is lost in that which you desire. You will attain to nothing by force of wishes, rather by force of arms. He who seeks to be thanked seeks enemies. He who is thirsty, having drunk, turns his back on the fountain. The cloud that the sun has raised obscures that same sun. The more gently you handle the nettle, still it pricks. The pig does not raise his eyes to him who throws him acorns. In loose mouths the news grows like soaked wheat. Señor, there are those who would sell the sun, and (like Tiberius) charge rent for urinals. But I am satisfied that those who flatter, gossip; that he who can hold out no longer resorts to his teeth. There is none who practices giving save the glutted and the dead. That the pig yields no profit until Saint Martin's. Many raise themselves up by their own weight, not like palm trees, but tumbler toys: I find but one thing mete in this world, that she who wears cork sandals should be stockinged in bark. From the evil, least. Upon wooden clogs passes the honor of man. There are fine gentlemen who eat cold, since hot is for the vulgar, and galled ass, that because of the flies has a wisp of twigs tied to his tail. The harridan cloaks her folly in plumes, as she tries to muster strength to hide the dread in her breast. Long sleeves enter the platter first. All goes to the point. Stains come out by rubbing, and there is no door will creak once the hinges are greased. The old man redyes himself with *malpica*[20] and wishes us to believe that it is a miracle, and not from pickled fish. All wish to be less good than famous, and few fear conscience as they do fame. They look for virtue not in themselves, but others: only that which is profitable do they hold to be just. As humans, they flatter themselves with being human. They make no excuse for desiring that which they may not (nor should) have. Without loving they desire to be loved, and praised where there is lacking a free hand. Know, then, that the bees never go to a faded flower, and that men without virtue are like money without its stamp. We all know that time and straw ripen medlars. That to him who knows how to wait, all comes pat. That the loon builds a house and breaks a young filly for another. That every ant has his shelter, and then is lost like woman, when he grows wings. That the lining of good service is solid hatred. That lacking a coat, a mending suffices; and that saintly poverty has no other benefits than to merit all, and to despise everything. We know also that those who feel for all things never lack headaches. That there is no need for huntsman to marry a butterfly. That everyone laughs at the monkey and he at them all. That the estate is not his who owns it, but his who enjoys it. That there is nothing more longwinded than to plant palm trees, begin a lawsuit, and wait till an old man dies. That the devil loves his own. Also we may be assured that the bird Phoenix, the song of the swan, seeds of the fern, sirens of the sea, ghosts, the truth, the shadow of the Marquez de Villena,[21] and Juan de Espera en Dios,[22] amount to the same thing as good fortune. The tale about San Amaro,[23] and the little story of the soul of Traxano.[24] I'd rather eat boots well stewed than truths raw. All is semblances. To whip a shadow. To grasp the wind. To plow water, and before the end of a year the prophecy comes up. The sexton never hears Mass. Big thieves punish the little ones, fishes the same. The follies of the rich are measuring rods. This sets wisdom back on its heels, like one coming downstairs. And in putting down his foot discovers his brain. That is known by his wife, with whom he gets more than obstinacy. The clerk figures the will on his finger nails, by which he would seize it, after the rule of *uñero, uñero, para mí me lo quiero*[25]—by dint of grasping I would have it for my own. This other who dies, loads up the funeral with mourning and singers, though he has nothing for Mass and goes plugged with tow, since what more do I care? Others leave their mark of friendship imprinted on the hand, cat fashion. There is a great to-do; since the ass has run away, they take vengeance on the packsaddle. And whim, that would make up for lack of bread by Christmas carols. Between two chairs, one falls to the floor, and another runs to make love to the widow at the funeral of her late lamented. Many appear fat as poodle dogs that die of pure hunger. What would Your Grace wish me to say save that all that, that is the world, is his own, pure and simple?

Those that war on me are the doctors, bullies from the page of the book of death, and they preserve me better, those fellows, than pickles. There is no poniard so polished as their prescriptions. The rings on their fingers display the plunder they have taken from those they bring low. Horse trappings for mourning. Thus they plunge into a Christian body, as into a cistern, and remove the life at so much cash. To all they make themselves out to be sacred. By this mules go wrong, as well as cures. I saw S. D. F. Quevedo in a dream, into whom *several doctors were entering on the backs of mules, which, with their black trappings, looked like so many tombs wearing ears. Their gait was absentminded, boresome and broken, in such sort that the duennas drew about all atitter, rocking back and forth like sawyers, their aspect filthy from so much gazing into urinals and chamber pots: their mouths so masked in beards, scarcely could you discover a pug nose, habited like cowherds: gloves soaking in an infusion, doubled up like him they

* Here begins Quevedo's passage, nearly verbatim, from his "Sueño de la muerte" (Vision of Death).—JC

would work upon. Big ring on the thumb, with so huge a stone that when they take the pulse it prognosticates a tombstone for the sick. Such they were in great numbers, and all came spouting platitudes together. Who, following the schools lackey-like, and having to do more with mules than with learning, graduate as physicians, and seeing them, I said: If out of such as these they make those, how will those others undo us? About them gathered a great rabble and throng of druggists (patience, my enemies), with spatulas unsheathed and syringes in the socket, armed with suppositories and plasters, from top to toe. The drugs they sell (even if they are decaying in the vial from pure age, and the poultices have cobwebs on them) they give out for recently cut from the piece; and such are their subtle medicines. The outcry of him who is dying begins with the brass mortar of the pharmacist, goes on to the lively march of the surgeon-barbers, passes by to the clapping of the gloves of the medico,[26] and finishes with the ringing of church bells. There are no men so fierce as druggists: they are the doctors' armorers: they give them their weapons; there is nothing of theirs that does not pertain to the miseries of war nor allude to offensive weapons. Sweet drinks (*jarabes*), which have rather too many letters for darts (*jaras*), than a lack of them. Needles, to mention those with a sting. Spatulas are swords in their language. Pills are bullets. Enemas and potions, cannon; and thus we have the canons of Medicine; and properly observed, to touch upon the delicate subject of purges, they are from the shops of hell: the sick, the damned: the doctors, the devils: and it is certain, that doctors are like devils, since one and all, they follow after the sick and reign over the well, and all their desire is, that the good, the well, shall be sick—that is evil, and the sick (the evil), never more well. They came all habited in prescriptions, crowned with Rx-Rx arrow thrusts, with which they begin their prescriptions; and I noticed that the doctors talked to the apothecaries, saying: *Récipe,*[27] which is to say: receive. In the same manner a mother talks to her daughter, and cupidity to the Public Minister. There is nothing else in the prescription but Rx-Rx arrow thrusts for the sinful, and later *ana, ana,*[28] which together make Ananias, and Cayafas, to condemn a just man. There follow ounces, and more ounces. What solace with which to flay a sick lamb! Later they string out numbers of simples that seem invocations to devils. Duphtalmus, Opoponax, Leotopilatum, Tragoricanum, Potamogetum, Henopugino, Petrocilinum, Scisa, Rapax, and Vinix. To know what those threats or hurly-burly of voices signify, so full of big letters, they are carrots, radishes, and parsley and other dirty things of the same sort. And as they have heard it said that he who does not know you buys you, they disguise the vegetables, that they may not be recognized, and the sick buy them. *Eglomatis,* they say, is syrup. *Catapoia,* pills. *Clister,* medicine. *Balanos,* a suppository. And the names of their prescriptions are so numerous, and so many their drugs, that most often from disgust of the nastinesses and stenches with which they pursue the sick, the illness flies off; for, what pain is there, of such bad taste, that it will not flee out of the marrow bones, rather than keep a Guillén Zervén plaster in place, and the leg or thigh see itself transformed into a blister? When I looked on these things, and on the doctors, I understood how improper (to note a difference) is that disgusting saying: Much passes between the pulse and the bum. For, in the first place, nothing passes, and only the doctors pass; for immediately following the pulse they go to the pot and the urinal to question of them that which they do not of themselves know the answer, for Galen sent them to the stool and the urinal, and as if the urinal would speak to their sense of hearing, they raise it to the ear, slavering their beards with its vapors. What a sight it is, seeing them go about to come to an understanding, by signs, with the stool, to take their thoughts from the great pot, and their words from the stench of it? You wouldn't expect it of the devil. O cursed inquisitors against life, for they choke with the tourniquet, slaughter with bleedings, bruise with cups, and disinter souls; for they lift them from the earth of their bodies, lacking soul, and without conscience! After, follow the surgeons loaded with pinchers, and probes, cauterizing irons, scissors, razors, saws, hacks, pliers, and lancets. Among them I heard a very dolorous voice, which said: Cut, pull, open, saw, break to pieces, stab, puncture, slice, tear away, and burn. It filled me with fear, the more so to see the tattoo they performed with the cautery irons and probes. Divers of my bones sought to creep within themselves for terror. I shrank into a heap. About that time there appeared a number of demons bearing chains of molars, and other teeth, forming trusses; by this I knew they were tooth pullers, the trade most accursed in the world, since it has no use but to depopulate mouths and hasten old age. These eat with the teeth of others, and see no tooth they would not prefer on their string, than in its proper jaw. They mistrust the people of Saint Apollonia,[29] bring suits against the gums, and quarry mouths. I never had so bad a moment as I had in seeing their forceps. They go after the teeth of others as if they were rats and ask money for pulling a molar as though they were putting it in. Who would come accompanied by such an accursed rabble, I said, and it seemed to me that the devil was small matter compared with such an evil crew. When I heard a great noise of guitars approaching, I felt a little cheered. All were playing lively music, passacalles, and bacanalles. May they kill me if it be not the surgeon-barbers, and they entering in. It was not difficult to tell that these people have passacalles infused into them, and the guitar as a natural gift. It was something to see the ones pluck and the others scrape the strings. I said to myself: Sore of beard, he who is mated with a grasshopper will see himself shaved, and be bled from the arm, going through chaconnes and merry dances, so to come finally to the conclusion that all those most gracious ministers of the martyrdom of death were hard up for cash, penny officials, and old iron and that only the barbers saw any silver, forthwith I was intrigued to watch a beard shaved and a raw sheepskin tanned.*

But inasmuch as neither friends nor enemies are good witnesses, let us change the subject. What profit, lovely wife, if it be a question of jail? Pull one foot from the mire and sink in with the other. What distinction is it to spit blood on a golden carpet? What worth to darken with antimony eyelids already dark? What prudence, to loose the dogs and tie the stones? What devotion, to pray to a saint only until the river is crossed?

---

* Here ends Quevedo's passage.—JC

What hurry, to flee on stilts? What stew, if the egg lack salt? I asked recently of a huntsman: Whither away? He replied: We're out to kill God's mercy. Said a master of etymologies (a gift of Masonry), salt pork in the pan says *chi*,[30] and the mistress says, *menea*[31] (turn it); from that is derived *chimenea*[32] (chimney). Before she buried her husband, I saw a widow ask for soup out of the pot, and wine, in order to be able to weep when the friars should come.

    • One should not put one's trust in a Baptist Nun (*Monja*

• *After another sheaf of proverbial advices growing more and more stringent as the narrative goes on: "One should not put one's trust in bulky letters, in golden hair by word of a poet, red lips and blue eyes, in long-lived prosperity." We find among the rest, "Coward, I don't want money to be a man's tool, but a man must have money." You can well imagine Quevedo speaking there. "A woman and a pane of glass, in a trice."*

The author as if Quevedo at this point begins to talk generally with considerable feeling. His advice is serious and reflects as much upon Quevedo himself and his present state as the world. It begins to hurt, and Quevedo is more than half himself the butt of it as the author goes on:

"But inasmuch as the file wastes itself in taking hold . . . Don't, don't, don't . . ." and then, his speech becoming more and more vulgar and more vague, if weightier, to the point in impact, he begins his final passage with "Fop. Let's not beat about the bush." Then comes the bang. A brawl. "Pell-mell" and we are in it. Then for nearly three full pages, to the end, we are taken up by something, something happening, tantalizing in its obscurity, that gives us the denouement of this inappropriate liaison.

It is not a composition in obscurity only but in lowness—suitable to the occasion, as our author would have us believe. He descends to the level—a pure literary device—of those he attacks. He has come to his climax, the point he would make, the climax of his scurrility and of his story—his deliberate scurrility as a gossip and an inspired clown.

He sails in. Only the lowest would be congruous here, the crass (if sparkling) language of the riffraff of that day will serve now. And thus he lets you know what he thinks of such servants of Church and State as those of whom he is speaking—who have found their despicable level beside hold-up men, pimps, and snatch-purses.

Baptista) who celebrates the feast day with puff cakes. Nor in a widower who remarries, for he gives himself away. Nor to walk mincingly. Nor to talk with a lisp. Red lips, and blue eyes. Butter in the bonnet to soften Pharaoh, being better than oil of bricks. In foibles of the vain, the complexion boxes of ugly women. In bulky letters. In saints of an image vendor. In him who has been forced upon religion. In golden hair, by word of a poet. In love that quarrels, like a winter's sun. In hard looks, from a bowman cloaked in a mantle, nor waiting in anterooms to reach a salon. In the skill of a poor man. In the strength of a drudge. In the turn of dice. In long-lived prosperity. In a summer cloud. In the serenity of winter. In mother-in-laws' scraps. In the scruples of a pious woman. In a house newly built. In a green innkeeper. In the visitant image vendor. In the virginity of a vagrant. In bread out of the bin. In faggots of pumpkin vine. In a clumsy scholar. And wine kept in a jug. To trust, to confide, and to contradict. In a man full of odd quirks. In a woman who lives all places but in her own home, and in her who puts aside cloth from which to cut herself a habit. My noble friend, one night you are the stick, the next the candle? Merchant, you keep the coffer hid in the dark, as if it were truth? Young student, who demands by the glove, your case is backed by a cruller vendor. Simple saint (though full of guile), bless not my yawns for sighs, that you may know where you sit. Vain one, do you not know that in every long lineage there are magistrates and tavern keepers? You that believe in everybody, he will dine with you who believes himself somebody. Sir Gallant, fine clothes will cover a poor lineage. Hypocrite, believe me, impossible to get about, when the muleteer is sending up thanks to God. Gossip, the oven grows hot at the mouth. Favorite, there above, in the heights is learned the loftiness of the mason builder, and the healthiest dies among the first. Old toothless hag, don't go to weddings, but to funerals. Officer of the Law, don't send us to seek Justice, and yield up the purse. Windy consoler, bring oil if you want to cry all night, for he plays safe who calls for a fire. Sick man, that promised to go and eat turkey at the hermitage, why do you gulp down so much of it, that you make yourself sick again? Pretender, unless you want to leak water, see that you don't lack pitch. Fearful, look that your little finger doesn't soil itself in the plate, like the rest, out of timidity, and let each seek his own fortune. Coward, I don't want money to be a man's tool, but a man must have money. Pieface, if you don't know how to put up an argument, marry; but remember that a borrowed pig makes a good winter and a bad summer. You are aware, of course, that woman must make three trips from home: to the baptismal, the altar, and the sepulchre. And that she has four virtues: to raise complaints, lie thoughtlessly, go where she pleases, and weep without cause. It is not enough to be chaste to be good. A woman and an orange, as smooth as you please. A woman and a pane of glass, in a trice. A woman and a mule for coaxing. Soup and dalliance come first. A vessel and a girl taste of the first thing that is put into them. Love of woman and fire of furze light well and are gone. The flower of the almond, the day that it opens, fades. A beautiful woman makes short shrift of her husband's good name. Wine from a decanter, good in the morning, vinegar by night. Remember also, brother, that though love can do much, money does it all. To iron lock, there is ever a passkey of silver. Don't wish for a potter's oven as a neighbor. Watch out that for want of knife they don't shove a stave in the sheath. It is of no importance to play well if you lose. Smoke speaks of fire. Shivaree brings money, love, and a cough. A donkey loaded with gold climbs to the rooftop. Caution avoids horns. Finally, if the aforementioned be gracious, dress her in clear blue of the sky, or May weather. If she should desire gambols, make it those of a dancer. If a little present, something of Martha the pious. If requitals, a stolen chain. If she be mad, wind her up. And if good (in spite of their redness), best is to profit by the golden occasion of her tresses.

But inasmuch as the file wastes itself in taking hold, I would witness for myself what misfortune it is to the rich man who in himself is poor. That which concerns me, I must pursue it; and since V. M. has taken your doctorate at the palace in the canons of good taste, I ask that you make some proofs of me, to reform my habits because the vulgar smell worse than the slippers of an innkeeper.

Chorumbo replied: Does Your Grace wish that I sell honey to the dealer in comb and that I preach to him during Lent? *Santa mía*,[33] the line drawn between brothers is a good thing. But in order that obedience not lessen our strength, let it be rather a command, and that he who errs by obedience shall not lose merit by erring. I will fold the paper and cast the scissors aside, come what may.

You, whoever it may be who wishes not to be a well-mule, that walks and walks, and gets nowhere, fly from coarseness in your conversation, for you will be no less hated than if you were evil. Keep your head level, not to resemble a gourd in the wind. Don't keep your arms dangling like the sleeves of a coat. Don't fix your eyes on the faces of others, as if you were praying. Don't stand so near that you blow on him like a quack. When you bridle, don't froth up, like a mule in an entryway, nor spit like a sprinkler of holy water, nor stick your hands in your pockets, like a page with the itch. Don't muffle yourself up like the young lady from Denmark, nor play with a key on the finger, like one who winds up thread, nor with the feet like a horse that has fleas, nor with the hands like a sheep shearer, nor wipe your nose with the bare fist, making a handkerchief of it, nor stroke your beard as if you were a cat, nor make your moustaches the strings of a bass fiddle, nor your gloves tablets of San Lázaro,[34] nor beat the measure with your hand like a choirmaster, nor cut quills, like Maese Pedro,[35] nor belch aloud, that San Antón[36] take you for a pig, nor sniffle so, that you will become a nuisance, nor make bird shot with the wax from your ears, even if it be with good intention, nor bullets of what you take from your nostrils, to kill a Christian, nor eat with both cheeks full, to look like "wind" on the almanac, nor when you yawn, show the grinders of the dragon nor end the story hee-hawing, that a donkey not answer you, nor take the hand of him to whom you are talking, because you are not going to marry him, nor tap him on the chest as if sanctifying him, nor handle his clothes like a tailor, who tests the weave, nor finger the buttons of patience, nor talk in the throat like a turkey, nor hum with the lips like a grandmother who rambles on, nor talk to yourself, for you will have a crackbrained audience, nor grind your teeth to give emphasis, nor laugh so loud, that they can see your liver, nor climb two steps at a time, that you look like a man without a head, nor throw one leg over the other, like the figure four, nor exaggerate, nor in order to say that they have given you nothing, thumb your nail to your teeth, like one who bites into the leaf of the wild artichoke, nor wipe your sweat on your napkin, if you are not already taken for a sloven. When you chew, don't sputter. When you say goodbye, don't bow too much, nor take yourself off sheepishly, nor harbor a spirit of resentment. Don't dispute everything like a mother-in-law. Don't be stubborn, for you will be hated. Nor finical, like a woman after childbirth. Don't act the clown, nor tell what you have dreamed, nor speak of the charms of your wife, nor of your children. Don't be ceremonious, nor funny out of a book, nor pride yourself on being supremely happy. When others laugh, don't pull a long face, nor bite your fingernails, nor spit big, nor strut, nor make mocking gestures with the hands. * Avoid vulgar expressions, evil sounding, low, of foul meaning,

---

* *As the pace quickens, the author says—descending to the dregs of speech—"This way you must never write," and from here on leaps to the attack; at the very end, an orgy of jazz counterpoint: unfortunately lost to precise sense but, still, wonderfully, generative of excitement as the words pile up, zippy zappy, and we glimpse a scene in a garden, a walled garden. There we see an old man with a dyed beard, a church dignitary, near to the court, and his kept woman, a girl of barely fifteen years.*

Also, of course, a young man. Outside the garden wall it is time of fiesta and mirth. It is peaceful in the garden, where the young "wife" is idling under the watchful eye of her "keeper."

The old boy must have lost sight of her for a moment. Is it night? It must be night. The lights and music of the fiesta reach to the girl. Has the old man fallen asleep? Of course.

Suddenly he wakes and senses the event. He gropes through the paths of the garden,

impertinent, indecorous, lacking gallantry, obscure in meaning, as in allusion, for with them you will no less sully yourself than by vagueness in our speech, as we say, silly pated. Fop. Let's not beat about the bush. A brawl. Pell-mell. An interloper. In season and out. A bungler. To hatch endless lies. Without so much as your leave, and may love never pain me. He told him everything from A to Z. The old tight fist, he keeps a sharp eye on her. There was neither track nor trace. To the hoof, the prairie. Face to face. Presto! just like that. There was no quarrel between Goldy and the Moor. Torquemada and his ass.[37] God decrees what shall happen. A double-crosser. Denied it boldfaced. Obdurate. At every tic. He flies into a rage. With his sheep's belly. To what end these sinecures? Laid upon the thorn of Santa Lucía.[38] Hot foot. The pool danced before him. On the spot. Mahomet in Granada. *Tocar a Abenámar.*[39] Long, long since. The other said. Fifty-fifty. Keep by me, Your Grace. As I tell it. This my version: Your Grace follows me. Continue, Your Grace, with the reading.

(cont.) *calls out and gets no answer. The noise of the carnival. Distracted, going about in the dark all at once*—pardicas!—*he steps upon the back of something live in his way and falls.* Chinfarrada. Percox. *A wild chase ensues through trees whose low branches catch his beard.*

Over the wall! Moor or Christian. He takes his child-wife to task, drags her indoors. She smoozles him in the most brazen style. Seduces him skillfully • but what will the event prove nine months hence?

Or do I go too fast? What, for our author?

Here the pure literary man indulges his muscles and peeled senses—indulges in a grand spree—"never write like this." Alas, that we cannot follow him fully. So he takes leave of us and of his patron—who presumably knew fully and in detail what he was talking about.

Don't try to keep up with me. I have my slab on the roller. Sealed with gum of the rockrose. God, and congratulations. Wall and a half. A lad like a golden pine tree. He drinks the winds. Let him who is most able carry the cat to the river. *Todo es agua de cerrajas.*[40] A bolt, in and out. He put his breast to the waves. Took it to heart. Barren thunder. Pigheaded. A moon as bright as midday. Dark as the mouth of a wolf. A hideout. A downpour. A whore's life. A higher bid. A wild clatter. *Barquinazo.*[41] A heavy fall. She arrived as if caught unawares. He, as though shot from a gun. They let each other have it. No straw smoke to his talk. A full-faced man. To the very black of the nails. Gripes. *En el pelo de la masa.*[42] Right to the bottom. So melancholy of virtue. He would walk on the tips of cresses. *Por quítame allá esa paja.*[43] In the twinkling of an eye. At every stir. To go round about. He takes devious ways. Don't drive me mad. He seized heaven in his arms. Face to face. I don't know how the devil to say it. He went straight to the point. A hard bargainer. Merrymaking. The streets festooned. Wide open. Spread apart. Unbraced. Windy. In a funk. *Repantigado.*[44] Stretched at ease. He went headlong. Burst forth. Give the boy credit. Turn about. Just stumbled on him. Sent him to hell and gone. Solid and upstanding. Enough said. Quit now. *Pardicas.*[45] He lit out. Followed like an old nag. Unlucky born. Gave him aplenty. Nothing to me. Stop. Rather my lips to the wall. Completely pooped. Crumbs in a friar's cowl. I don't know a thing. Scattered the bloom. Tore it to shreds. Hedged. A fine bore we have. Nightlong undecided. Cut himself off. Stargazing. Pretending not to see. Nothing for it but to be patient. Kept like gold in a sack. Full of airs. Deceits. He allows himself to be cozened. One and another showed their contempt. He is in a dilemma. I stick to it. Two to one. *Tabahola*.[46] *Tahanero*.[47] At each other's throats. People began to whisper it about. With such angry mien. Merrymaking. I won't give in. Got the cold shoulder. Pled with God, that He reform her. As if he had been a novice. This is the finish. A scuffle. An upstart. He goes grumbling. To another more stiff jointed. Neither king nor castle. In truth, how he loosed his tongue. He tells what must be done and what will happen. Not the place or time for it. Added this to that. Offered it at a bargain. At the last minute. All messed up. I don't trust him; he's shifty. Not a word. He was cagey. Never, nevermore. No class. Double-crosser. Cheap stuff. Complaints. Set. Harebrained. With good reason. Muling and puling. Sliced meat aplenty. A frown. A radish. On your guard. Another tack. This and that. Barter. Begone. Pugh. Caresses. Enfeebled. Skinny. Pigheaded. A botcher. With all his might. Tricks of a charlatan. Hollabaloo. Braggart. Worn-out. Benumbed. Rattlebrained. On his knees. Bluster. The basket of Ines. Let's laugh with Ines. The son of Mari Buttock. *La gata de Mari Ramos*.[48] Shut up. Crafty. Balky. Look at me. Strut about. Fop. Glutton. Blowhard. Windbag. Shaking all over. Delicacies. A litter. Bursts of laughter. Rage. Sallies and retorts. Urgings. Pawed her up. Rocked. In tears. *Chinfarrada*.[49] A great racket. A sudden onset. Uproar. Roughly handled. In a heap. There it is. They fell flat. Backward. Waddling about. All of a sudden. *Percox*.[50] Bewitched. Crooked. Clawings. To hang the head. A petty vulture. Hatred. Provided you don't look. As per usual. Tidbits. Goofily. Made a face at him. With clothes tucked up. Come-ons. Clicked. Lazy. Spite. Got by deceit. Beat it. Come what may. Let happen what will. After a time. To stall. To get burnt. A speech. Like a peevish child. Chisler and smoosh and other vulgarisms of the sort.

At this a noise sounded, and in order not to be seen, I moved on. God keep Your Excellency et cetera.

Notes

These notes are intended to clarify selected names and also to provide the meanings of various foreign words, phrases, and proverbs that appear in the translation. The novella invites hundreds of notes, but in keeping with Williams's wish that this book not be a "scholarly exhibit" (*Autobiography*), just the following are offered here:

1. *Chorumbo* means "spot" (stain); it is a regional synonym for *churrete*. Its auditory association with *chumbo*, slang for "prick," is of possible significance. Another possibility of meaning is the association with the Portuguese word *chorume*, which means "overflowing" and, in this case, implies "runs at the mouth." The working title of the novella, prior to its publication, was *Chorumbo*.

2. Don Gonzalo is a figure in many old Spanish proverbs. In the legend of Don Juan, he is the father of a seduced girl, and he is killed by Don Juan in a fight over her.

3. La Bermuda (in English, Bermuda) is the main island of the group discovered by Juan Bermúdez in 1527, and its waters were associated with multiple dangers, including pirates and hurricanes, thus its association with making the sign of the cross.

4. Juan Barbón (lit. John Beard) represents an unwary, innocent man and alludes to the bearded hermits of the Carthusian order.

5. Laurencio Vala (Lorenzo Valla, 1407–57) is an Italian humanist, philosopher, and literary critic; his *Elegantiae linguae Latinae* (Elegances of the Latin Language) was the first textbook of Latin grammar written since late antiquity, and it became popular in grammar schools throughout Europe. He also was considered a bogeyman for questioning a document seen as undergirding the papacy's legitimacy.

6. Barbarroja (1475–1546) is a famous Turkish pirate, known in English as Red Beard.

7. Doctor Sumo Campo is a priest whom, it is thought, Espinosa had actually heard give the sermon described here, and whom he calls loco (crazy) in the original Spanish version.

8. *Oliva, olivo, y azeytuno, y todo es uno* literally means "olive, olive tree, and olive fruit, and all are one and the same"; the proverb is equivalent to the vulgarized Shakespeare: a rose by any other name is still a rose.

9. *Porro unum est necessarium* (Luke 10:42) is Latin, meaning "but one thing is needed."

10. *Cañarí* is an old Andalusian word that literally means "like a reed" and thus hollow and weak. The Spanish text says *caballero cañarí*, or "wimpy knight."

11. Viscaya, a province in the Basque Country of Spain, is famous for its iron mines dating back to Roman times.

12. A "twenty-four" (*veinticuatro*) is an archaic term denoting a municipal official.

13. *Blanca y cornado* are the names (lit. white and horned) of ancient coins, both considered small change.

14. Alkoran is the Quran, commonly called the Koran.

15. Galen is the Greek physician whose theories formed the basis of European medicine until the Renaissance.

16. Pero Ganso (lit. But Goose/Simpleton) is a popular folk character in old Spanish proverbs.

17. *Pater familias* is Latin for the father of a family and refers to a man who is the head of a household.

18. *Gongorize* implies saying something with an affected diction and style, and here it is intended in the context of the controversy between Quevedo and Góngora over *conceptismo* and *culteranismo*, respectively.

19. Lilibeo, known today more widely as Marsala, is a seaport town in western Sicily, Italy.

20. *Malpica* is a lotion for dying hair, according to Francisco López Estrada.

21. Marquez de Villena is a legendary figure who made a pact with the devil, promising to surrender his soul at death in return for having every wish fulfilled during his lifetime. For a time he outwitted the devil by prolonging his life indefinitely, but eventually succumbed, as dark deeds cannot remain hidden forever.

22. Juan de Espera en Dios is the legendary wandering Jew, poor and begging for small change, who lives for centuries.

23. San Amaro (Saint Amaro), in medieval legend, is an abbot and sailor who sailed across the Atlantic to an earthly paradise.

24. Traxano is a legendary figure who, though never baptized, led a virtuous life. His soul was saved as a result of his great goodness.

25. *Uñero, uñero, para mí me lo quiero* literally means "ingrown nail, ingrown nail, I would have for myself"; the idea behind the proverb is take all one can grab.

26. Medico means "physician," and it is a direct import from Spanish.

27. *Récipe* means "prescription of a physician."

28. *Ana* is an abbreviation put on prescriptions to signify an equal amount of ingredients.

29. Saint Apollonia is the patron saint of dentistry and those suffering from toothaches or other dental problems.

30. *Chi* (pronounced chee) is an onomatopoeia, as in the sound of frying salt pork.

31. *Menea* literally means "move back and forth" or "shake."

32. *Chimenea* actually derives from the Old French *cheminée*, meaning "smoke vent," not as described in the mock etymology in the novella.

33. *Santa mía* literally means "my saint" (female) and is used as an interjection, equivalent in English to "my goodness," and so on.

34. San Lázaro is Saint Lazarus, whose tablets here are associated with collecting alms for chapels and shrines.

35. Maese Pedro is Master Pedro, the character in *Don Quixote* who has a puppet show and who is an impostor in his own life.

36. San Antón (Saint Anthony) is the patron and protector of the lower animals and particularly of pigs; he was a swineherd before he became a saint.

37. Torquemada is a folkloric figure who sold water carried by

his donkey. The expression "Torquemada and his ass" describes a person who has an inseparable dull companion.

38. The "thorn of Santa Lucía" (Saint Lucy) means the "pangs of hunger." While the derivation of this figure of speech remains obscure, it has been associated with the sword that killed her.

39. *Tocar a Abenámar* literally means "touching Abenámar," the central character in *The Romance of Abenámar*, a medieval Spanish romance written as a dialogue between the Moor Abenámar and the Catholic King John II of Castile.

40. *Todo es agua de cerrajas* literally means "all is sow thistle water"; the expression means "good for nothing" or "nothing but empty words."

41. *Barquinazo* means a "bump," "jolt," "tumble," or "hard fall."

42. *En el pelo de la masa* literally means "in the hair of the mass" and is a figure of speech that here means "plain and simple" or "in plain Spanish."

43. *Por quítame allá esa paja* literally means "because of that straw there being taken from me," implying a quarrel for a straw; here, the expression means "for no good reason." (It appears that Williams found "in the twinkling of an eye" in a Spanish-English dictionary of his day, given as the meaning of the related phrase, *en quítame allá esas pajas.*)

44. *Repantigado* means "stretched out" or "sprawled."

45. *Pardicas* (now *pardiez*) is an interjection that means "by God" or "by gad."

46. *Tabahola* means "din," as in the confused noise of a crowd.

47. *Tahanero* means "buttocks."

48. *La gata de Mari Ramos* literally means "the pussycat of Mari Ramos" (folkloric woman); the expression describes a person who aspires to something while pretending not to want it.

49. *Chinfarrada* means "jab" or "cutting remark."

50. *Percox* means "muck"; here, possibly in the vulgar slang sense, it is an interjection equivalent to "bullshit."

NOTA BENE: Clarification of the novella's subtitle and its translation is warranted. Espinosa called the work a *novela peregrina*, which Williams translated as "perambulatory novella." In a passage of his commentary not included in the present edition, he explains that *peregrina* has "the same root as peregrination: [Quevedo] was wandering about Spain at the time [of the novella's composition], in virtual exile." But the true author of the novella was living in Sanlúcar when he wrote it, not wandering about. How, then, was Espinosa describing his work? To answer this question, it is necessary to consider that *peregrina* can also mean "strange," "bizarre," "outlandish," etc. At the same time, the narrator says in his opening sentence that he was strolling—perambulating—when he encountered the Dog and the Fever. Readers are welcome to choose the translation most meaningful to them and their own reading of the novella.

The statements here, both private and public, reveal Williams's thoughts about and passion for this baroque novella from the point at which he began translating it with his mother during the Spanish Civil War, as well as the evolution of his involvement with it and his dogged determination to publish it:

Me Mother is helping me translate an old book I think it was you left here once: *El Perro y la Calentura*, by Quevedo [Williams is referring to his 1736 edition, which Pound had given him].
—Letter to Ezra Pound, 1936 (*The Selected Letters of William Carlos Williams*)

I hope it will be what I want it to be, but the test will come in the writing or assembling. The continuity will be difficult to manage along with the fluidity which I am determined to preserve. . . . The translation is showing up a curious old script that is something entirely new to me. . . . Innuendo, scandal, double meaning, obscenity, filth, contempt for woman, peasant humor, proverbs, anti-clericalism are blended into a hodge-podge of soup, goats, chamber pots until Gertrude Stein seems a simple, quiet mind beside them.
—Letter to Louis Zukofsky, 1937 (*William Carlos Williams and Louis Zukofsky*)

Geez, how I'd like you to use [in a *New Directions in Prose and Poetry* anthology] some of the novella . . . I've been translating, 1627 [*sic*] stuff, right on the ball. I could give you anywhere from twenty to forty pages or more if you had room for it. Maybe ten pages would be enough—the only difficulty being that unless the whole business is offered, it might be too puzzling for the ordinary reader to get the drift of it. I'm using the whole novella as a framework to hang my mother's biography on. Probably best not to fool with it now.

—Letter to James Laughlin, 1939 (*William Carlos Williams and James Laughlin: Selected Letters*)

It is written not only in old Spanish but in the most colloquial, slangy Spanish of that day. Some of the words I cannot find anywhere, even in the New York Public Library dictionaries—such a word, for instance, as *tablaoa* [i.e., *tabahola*]. . . . The last page is terrific! Not only does [the author] use the most difficult words but he goes out of his way to make the meaning as obscure as possible—of a purpose to do so to hide the meaning from the reader—the true meaning.

—Letter to Pedro Salinas, 1940, Houghton Library, Harvard University

[It is] far more "modern" than ever Hemingway or even Gertie ever thought of being. . . . It is absolutely "new directions" in its manner of writing and hot as hell besides. . . . Yep, it's double talk, early seventeenth century: the first recorded use of the pure image to tell a story. The story is that some old, long-nosed bastard, a high dignitary of the church, got some young gal in a family way—or married her or what not. But in the end she took up with some young blade who leaped the wall during carnival to lay her in the garden.

—Letters to James Laughlin, 1945, Houghton Library, Harvard University

There is a modern quality about it that is rather startling when the realization first strikes the eye, very much a literary collage, to tell directly a hidden story, if you will, without other explanation; almost a contemporary pastiche of words, proverbs, and phrases piled up, often with very little reference to syntax. . . . Apart from a sort of atomic bombardment of words as words, each carrying its own unrelated particle contributing to the meaning (while remaining themselves uninflected—a nice point), the practice represented speed. And it is speed that characterizes our contemporary scene.

—Introduction, "The Dog and the Fever," 1949, Beinecke Library, Yale University

Now get set for this one: I've never been satisfied to take your verdict on the . . . translation sitting down. It's got to appear between covers sooner or later. So I sat down, recently, and wrote me an introduction to the piece, stating why I think it is important, at least important enough to its printing. But that ain't all.

I have an idea all to myself concerning how the book should be set up. I want to run the script of the translation in a proper faced type from page to page continuously but not to fill the whole of the page, the lower part, less than half, of the page, under a line across the page, to be occupied by my introduction of comment on the text, a little on one page, more on the next or not any on certain pages, as the requirements of the text may determine.

Thus the translation of the text with its dedicatory letter will have preference over everything else; it will *not* be second to a long introduction like a Shaw play. On the other hand, the text, which is acknowledgedly difficult, will get the benefit of an explanatory running comment just below the sentences as they unfold.

—Letter to James Laughlin, 1949, Houghton Library, Harvard University

To me the novel is unique and fascinating. . . . The scheme of it is a putting down of the facts about the corrupt court, but not openly. . . . We have a story told in terms of proverbs of the people. . . . It is all by implication; nothing is directly stated—very much as might be done today. . . . Mother and I began the work casually, but before long we grew engrossed in it as we attempted to find in English equivalents for the old Spanish. . . . Someday I hope to make it attractive by doing a running commentary to accompany and interpret the text. I don't want a scholarly exhibit. I want something that can be read by anyone looking for amusement.

—*The Autobiography of William Carlos Williams*, 1951

PEDRO ESPINOSA (1578–1650) was a poet and fiction writer of the Spanish Golden Age (c. 1500–1650). As a young man, he established himself as a leading member of the famous school of poetry that arose in Antequera, the medieval town in southern Spain where he was born and raised. His education included both theology and canon law. He retreated to live as a hermit for three years after being bitterly disappointed in love, and subsequently, around 1613–14, he entered the priesthood of the Roman Catholic Church. In 1618 he entered the service of the Duke of Medina Sidonia and moved to Sanlúcar de Barrameda, a seaside town in the Cádiz province, in Andalusia, where he spent the rest of his life. He was given the position of chaplain in the ducal household and also rector of San Ildefonso School, which trained poor children in Spanish and Latin letters. In 1637 he retired from service of the duke. The modern Espinosa scholar Francisco López Estrada describes three main tendencies in both his poetry and prose: profane, religious, and panegyric. His prose works include several satires in the style of the fashionable *conceptismo* of his day. Another profane satire like *The Dog and the Fever* is his *Pronóstico judiciario* (Judicial Prediction), which ridicules astrology in a similar manner, with moralizing intent. He is best known in the history of early modern Spanish literature for his 1605 anthology of contemporary poets called

Las flores de poetas ilustres de España (Flowers of Spain's Illustrious Poets), which includes most of the important poets of the Golden Age. Of note, it is believed that he was a good friend of Francisco de Quevedo, who was first published in this anthology, and who became Spain's most famous practitioner of *conceptismo*. Espinosa included a section of Quevedo's satiric writing as an intercalation in *The Dog and the Fever*.

WILLIAM CARLOS WILLIAMS (1883–1963) is widely recognized as one of the greatest American poets of the twentieth century and as an influential founder of literary modernism. In addition to poetry, he authored works of fiction, criticism, drama, and translation. His importance to the development of modern American poetry grew out of his commitment to recording the "local" experience of Rutherford, New Jersey, and its environs, where he was born and raised, and where he subsequently settled and practiced medicine as a pediatrician and obstetrician. Among his most celebrated books are *Al Que Quiere!* (Four Seas), *Spring and All* (Contact; cited by the Library of Congress as one of the eighty-eight "Books That Shaped America"), *In the American Grain* (Albert and Charles Boni), *Paterson* (Books I–V; New Directions), and *Pictures from Brueghel and Other Poems* (New Directions), for which he posthumously received the Pulitzer Prize. He translated poetry and fiction from both Spanish and French, and he also translated classical Greek poetry (Sappho) and classical Chinese poetry. Concerning Spanish literature, Williams wrote in the late 1930s: "If more of the Spanish were better translated—more in the spirit of modern American letters, using word of mouth and no literary English—most of the principles which have been so hard-won, the directness, the immediacy, the reality of our present-day writing in verse and prose would be vitally strengthened. Our efforts away from vaguely derived, nostalgic effects so deleterious to the mind would be replaced by the directness and objectivity we so painfully seek." This vision of his is demonstrated in his translation of *The Dog and the Fever*. All told, during his lifetime Williams published some twenty books of poetry as well as seventeen books of prose—and he delivered more than three thousand babies.

RAQUEL HÉLÈNE (Rose Hoheb de) WILLIAMS (1847–1949), born and raised in Puerto Rico, was a would-be artist, Francophile, homemaker, and mother of William Carlos Williams. Her family history included Jews forced to flee Spain at the time of the Inquisition. Called Elena, she was half French and studied art in Paris at the Académie des Beaux-Arts in the late 1870s. Williams recounts this about his mother in his memoir, *Yes, Mrs. Williams* (New Directions): "She was no more than an obscure art student from Puerto Rico, slaving away at her trade, which she loved with her whole passionate soul, living it, drinking it down with her every breath—the money gone, her mother as well as her father now dead, she was forced to return with her scanty laurels, a Grand Prix, a few gold medals to disappear into a trunk in my attic." Elena's brother, Carlos Benjamin Hoheb, a surgeon after whom Williams was named, introduced her to his best friend, William George Williams. They were living in the Dominican Republic at the time, and a year later, in 1882, they were married. (Perfectly fluent in Spanish, William George would instill in his poet son a love of Spanish literature, and, during the period of World War I, they translated together works of poetry and fiction from Latin America.) Elena preferred French over Spanish, and in the late 1920s she assisted her son in translating from French Philippe Soupault's avant-garde novel *Last Nights of Paris* (Macaulay). It was at the urging of her son in 1936 that she assisted him in translating *The Dog and the Fever*.

JONATHAN COHEN (1949–) is an award-winning translator of Latin American poetry and scholar of inter-American literature. He is the compiler and editor of William Carlos Williams's *By Word of Mouth: Poems from the Spanish, 1916–1959*, and editor of the centennial edition of his *Al Que Quiere!*—both published by New Directions. Among his translations are *Pluriverse: New and Selected Poems*, by Ernesto Cardenal (New Directions); *Countersong to Walt Whitman and Other Poems*, by Pedro Mir (Azul Editions; reprinted by Peepal Tree Press); and *The Dark Room and Other Poems*, by Enrique Lihn (New Directions). Scholarly works include *A Pan-American Life: Selected Poetry and Prose of Muna Lee* (University of Wisconsin Press) and *Neruda in English: A Critical History of the Verse Translations and Their Impact on American Poetry* (Stony Brook University). For more information, visit jonathancohenweb.com.

PAUL MARIANI (1940–) is a widely acclaimed poet and scholar of British and American literature, with a specialization in twentieth-century poetry. He has published more than three hundred essays and reviews and is the author of eighteen books, with seven volumes of poetry and six biographies of master poets, including John Berryman, Robert Lowell, and Gerard Manley Hopkins. *William Carlos Williams: A New World Naked* (Norton) won the New Jersey Writers Award, was a National Book Award finalist, and was also named a *New York Times* Notable Book of the year. His biography of Hart Crane, *The Broken Tower* (Norton), was made into a feature-length film directed by and starring James Franco. His latest biography, *The Whole Harmonium: The Life of Wallace Stevens* (Simon and Schuster), appeared in 2016. He is university professor of English emeritus at Boston College.